Alessandro Serenelli
Murderer of St. Maria Goretti

A Story of Christian Redemption

Bret Thoman

Alessandro Serenelli
Murderer of St. Maria Goretti

A Story of Christian Redemption

Bret Thoman

Icona Press
Peachtree City, Georgia

Alessandro Serenelli, Murderer of St. Maria Goretti: A Story of Christian Redemption
by Bret Thoman

Copyright © 2024 by Bret Thoman.
All rights reserved.
Published by Icona Press: www.iconapress.com.
For permissions, contact: bret.thoman@gmail.com.

Cover design by Angie Alaya.
Cover Photograph courtesy of Capuchin convent of Macerata.

Scripture texts in this work are taken from the New American Bible, revised edition © 2010, 1991, 1986, 1970 Confraternity of Christian Doctrine, Washington, D.C. and are used by permission of the copyright owner. All Rights Reserved. No part of the New American Bible may be reproduced in any form without permission in writing from the copyright owner.

No part of this publication may be reproduced, stored in a retrieval system, or transmitted in any way by any means—electronic, mechanical, photocopy, recording, or otherwise—without the prior permissions of the copyright holder.

ICONA PRESS

This book is dedicated to all who have fallen and, through the Cross, have risen again.

CONTENTS

Author's Note 9
Timeline 11
Introduction: A Path toward Redemption 13
1: June 2, 1882 19
2: The Sea 24
3: Toward the Roman Countryside 29
4: Alessandro's Arrival 32
5: The Meeting of the Serenellis and Gorettis 35
6: The Pontine Marshes 38
7: The Cascina Antica 42
8: The Death of Luigi Goretti 46
9: How I Remember Her 49
10: A Portrait of Alessandro Serenelli 51
11: Dark Omens in the Cascina Antica 55
12: Darkness Descends 58
13: The Passion of Maria Goretti 61
14: The Final Encounter 66
15: The Death of a Saint 70
16: The Ferocity of Alessandro 73
17: Regina Coeli 77
18: The Motive 79
19: The Trial 87
20: Sentencing 91
21: Press Coverage 95
22: Assunta and the Aftermath 100

CONTENTS

23: The Dream	104
24: Life in Prison	108
25: Ongoing Conversion	112
26: Toward Freedom	118
27: The Difficult Return Home	124
28: Christmas in Corinaldo	129
29: It is my Duty to Tell the Truth	131
30: Alessandro's Mission	134
31: I Lied about Maria	137
32: Saint Maria Goretti	144
33: Return to the Cascina Antica	149
34: Towards the Convent	153
35: As a True Son of St. Francis	157
36: A Converted Man	160
37: Farewell to Mamma Assunta	164
38: The Testament	168
39: May 6, 1970	171
Appendix	177
The Prodigal Son	178
The Cross and Forgiveness	180
Stages of Forgiveness	182
Prayers of Forgiveness	185
Books by Icona Press	191
About the Author	193

Father, forgive them, they know not what they do.

Luke 23:34

Author's Note and Acknowledgement

I would like to thank Fr. Giovanni Alberti C.P. His book, *Alessandro Serenelli: Storia di un uomo "salvato"*, was invaluable for my own. Without it, this book would not have been possible.

Fr. Alberti is a Passionist priest and rector of the Sanctuary of Our Lady of Graces dedicated to Saint Maria Goretti, a journalist, and psychologist. Fr. Alberti is also the foremost authority on the life of Maria Goretti. In 1980, Fr. Alberti wrote the most complete biography on Maria Goretti (subsequently republished in numerous editions), followed by equally comprehensive books on the lives of Assunta Goretti and Alessandro Serenelli. Beyond his keen attention to detail and poetic writing style, the Christian spirit and Gospel message emanate from every page.

About ten years ago, I was privileged to spend two days with Fr. Alberti, in which I was the recipient of his boundless knowledge of the life of Maria Goretti and the "Gorettian" sites in and around Nettuno and Borgo Montello (formerly known as Conca). It was immediately obvious that he not only had a passion for the story of Maria Goretti, he had a heart for God.

During those two days, I was surprised to find myself struck by the other protagonist of the story. Alessandro Serenelli was not the monster I was judging him to be. While he committed an unspeakable act of ferocity against eleven-year-old Maria, like her, he, too, had been baptized, and his soul was indwelt by the grace of God. Moreover, he had endured numerous sufferings throughout his young life. It was difficult not to feel empathy for him, which soon progressed into compassion. While Alessandro Serenelli was the victimizer and not the victim, I could not escape being touched by his story.

As I learned more about Alessandro Serenelli, I began to be all the more gripped by his conversion, which began shortly into his thirty-year sentence in Noto, Sicily. After he was released, he chose to enter a religious community. Though he never took religious vows, he spent the last three decades of his life living essentially the same life as a Capuchin friar.

Alessandro Serenelli was a complex man with a complicated character. The young man who murdered a saintly girl in a fit of rage for not acquiescing to his carnal cravings was the same elderly man who died peacefully in the grace of God in a Franciscan infirmary. Alessandro's act reveals the fullness of the horror of sin. But equally reflected in him is the fullness of the mercy of God. His life trajectory, arced toward the goodness of God, reveals a truth: that no one—not even someone who has committed the most horrific sin—is beyond the redemption of God.

While the life of Maria Goretti is well-known, Alessandro's is still being discovered. It is my hope that this book will be a vessel of God's mercy and redemption.

Timeline

- June 2, 1882: Alessandro Serenelli is born in Paterno (Ancona) to Giovanni and Cecilia, the youngest of eight children.
- June 3, 1882: is baptized in the church of Santa Maria Assunta in Paterno.
- August 15, 1888: receives the Sacrament of Confirmation.
- March 26, 1890: Cecilia dies.
- October 16, 1890: Maria Goretti is born in Corinaldo
- 1894: The Serenelli family moves to Torrette, a fishing village near Ancona.
- 1894: Alessandro receives First Communion.
- June 20, 1897: Alessandro emigrates to Olevano Romano to work with his father, Giovanni.
- October 1898: The Serenelli father and son are introduced to the Gorettis; Alessandro meets Maria Goretti.
- February 1899: The Gorettis and Serenellis move to Le Ferriere di Conca in the Pontine Marshes.
- May 6, 1900: Luigi Goretti dies of malaria.
- July 5, 1902: After an attempted rape, Alessandro viciously attacks Maria Goretti, stabbing her fourteen times.
- July 6, 1902: Maria Goretti dies in a hospital in Nettuno.
- October 15, 1902: Is sentenced to 30 years in prison
- February 1903: Is sent to prison in Noto, Sicily.
- 1906 (toward the end of the year): Maria appears to him in a dream, initiating his conversion.
- Summer 1918: Is transferred to the penal colony in Augusta, Sicily.
- Spring 1919: Is transferred to Mamone (NU) prison in Sardinia
- 1924: Is transferred to Alghero prison in Sardinia.
- March 11, 1929: Is released from prison.
- March 21, 1929: Is reunited with his brother in Torrette.

- Christmas 1934: Goes to Corinaldo where he is forgiven by Mamma Assunta.
- 1936: Falls seriously ill with bronchopneumonia.
- 1937: Stays at the Capuchin sanctuary in Ambro-Amandola for several months.
- 1938–1956: Lives in the Capuchin friary in Ascoli Piceno.
- 1938–1941: Participates in Maria's canonization process in Albano.
- December 16, 1950: Returns to the Cascina Antica, where the murder took place.
- September 1954: Meets with Mamma Assunta (Maria's mother) the last time before her death.
- November 17, 1956: Is transferred to the Capuchin infirmary in Macerata.
- May 6, 1970: Alessandro Serenelli dies at the Capuchin infirmary in Macerata.

Introduction: A Path toward Redemption

Alessandro was born in Paterno (Ancona) on June 2, 1882, "the day Giuseppe Garibaldi died," as he later would recall. He was the last of eight children born to his father, Giovanni, and his mother, Cecilia. With the exception of Lucia, all his siblings died in tragic circumstances.

Alessandro has no memories of his mother, who died in a mental asylum when he was still a child. His older brother once told him that when he was an infant, she tried to throw him down a well. Shortly thereafter, she was committed. Alessandro had a brother who suffered from mental illness as well and was also committed. He suffered deeply due to the lack of a maternal role, and he would attribute some of the causes of his later transgressions to the absence of a mother.

His father Giovanni had an irascible character and was prone to drunkenness, leading to the loss of an important job as a foreman in Loreto. He moved around frequently while looking for work and took jobs as an agricultural laborer and sharecropper. Eventually, he became a courier, forcing him to be away from home frequently. As a result, Alessandro spent his childhood shuffled between a cousin's and an older brother's house. Despite his lack of parental figures, he attended school through the second grade and learned to read and write. But no one really looked after him.

When he was an adolescent, Alessandro's family was living in Torrette, a fishing village near Ancona. There, he found work as a sailor's assistant. While he was fascinated by the sea, it scared him, as he had never learned how to swim. Moreover, the sailors he spent most of his time with were known for their ill repute. These were his formative years.

Meanwhile, Alessandro's father and two older brothers had emigrated to an estate near Rome to work as sharecroppers, leaving Alessandro with his brother. After one of Giovanni's sons was hospitalized and another was drafted into the army, he sent his youngest son a letter asking him to join him in his work as a sharecropper. At the age of sixteen, Alessandro left the sea to join his father in the fields.

One year after his arrival, Giovanni was fired for arguing with his boss. Then, Alessandro and his father moved to Paliano to work as sharecroppers on another estate. Here, they came into contact with Luigi Goretti and his family, including his daughter Maria, and they agreed to a working relationship.

As a young man, Alessandro was exceedingly introverted. According to various testimonies, his favorite hobby was reading. He would immerse himself in magazines and periodicals, seeking to escape a world that must have appeared foreign and frightening to him. On the other hand, his frustrating family dynamic, the continuous change of residences and relationships, and possibly his family history of mental illness—surely, the death of his mother and brother in a psychiatric hospital affected his psychological development—accentuated his personality, described by his contemporaries as "taciturn, with schizoid traits."

After Giovanni argued with his new boss, once again his contract was terminated. Sadly, Luigi Goretti was fired as well. This time, the two families migrated to a small town called Le Ferriere di Conca, near Nettuno, some forty miles south of Rome. No one wanted to go. Conca was in the heart of the dreaded Pontine Swamps—a wild, marshy region infamous for brigandage and a haven for malaria. Yet they had no choice.

The two families were hired to work as sharecroppers on an estate owned by a wealthy nobleman named Count Mazzoleni. He provided them with a large farmhouse, known as the Cascina Antica, which they would share as if they were an extended family. The Goretti family lived on one side, while the Serenelli father and son resided on the other. A common kitchen separated the living quarters.

During this period, there was a familiar relationship between Alessandro and the Goretti children. Assunta considered him a nephew or even a son. Several times, she asked him to teach Maria to read, and Alessandro frequently accompanied the children into town to buy supplies from the dry goods store.

Sadly, Luigi Goretti died of malaria two years after arriving in Conca. This led to a spiral. Maria, though just ten years old, volunteered to take over her mother's roles, which involved caring for her younger siblings, cooking, and cleaning, while Assunta took her late husband's place working the fields.

After Luigi's death, the equilibrium that had existed between the two families deteriorated. Giovanni became possessive and dominant, lording his authority over his son, the Goretti widow, and her children. He began to drink more, and he forced Assunta and the children to assume more burdensome roles that should not have been theirs.

Alessandro, now twenty years old, became more reclusive and withdrawn. Worse, he began looking at eleven-year-old Maria differently. On two occasions, Alessandro made "immoral propositions." He even threatened her. Maria was horrified. Believing he was capable of violence, she was careful never to be alone with him. But Alessandro eventually devised a plan to force Maria into submission. He said, "After the second attempt, the resolution to succeed in venting my passion was formed more than ever, and I also conceived the idea of killing her if she continued to oppose my desires."

While Maria was seated on the landing at the top of the stairs and everyone else was outside working on the threshing floor, he planned to rape her. He placed an awl—a sharp farm tool used for picking ice or punching holes in wood—in a chest by the front door. With the excuse that he needed to take care of something in the house, he entered through the front door. Then he grabbed her by the arm and pulled her inside.

Maria resisted his intentions with all her strength. In a fit of rage, Alessandro took the awl and struck Maria fourteen times. Maria was brought to the hospital, where she died one day later. While she lay dying, she forgave Alessandro and declared that she wanted him to be with her in Heaven.

At his trial, Alessandro claimed that Maria had given her consent and that he stabbed her merely to be "cared for by the government." He also claimed mental illness, given that his mother and brother had been committed to an asylum. The jury did not heed his defense. Alessandro was convicted of three crimes—abuse of domestic relations, attempted rape, and premeditated murder— and sentenced to thirty years of imprisonment. Had he been twenty-one, he would have been sentenced to life without parole.

Alessandro served the first three years in isolation. Toward the end of this period, Maria appeared to him in a dream. She was walking in a garden, picking fourteen lilies and handing them to him one by one. At that point, he realized that she had forgiven him. He later said, "I woke up startled and said to myself, 'Now I, too, am saved, because I am certain that Marietta has come to visit me and to give me her forgiveness.' Since that day, I no longer felt the horror of my life as before."

After serving twenty-seven years (his sentence was reduced by three years for good behavior), he left a different man and went to live with a brother in Ancona, where he worked odd jobs. Shortly after his release, he went to Corinaldo and asked for the forgiveness of Maria's mother, Assunta. On December 25, 1934, he kneeled before her and said, "Forgive me, Assunta."

She replied, "If Maria has forgiven you, if God has forgiven you, then I, too, forgive you." The rest of her family also forgave him.

In another important moment, Alessandro testified at the ecclesiastical tribunal for Maria's canonization, correcting the false testimony he had given during his penal trial in Rome. He clarified that Maria had never given her consent and that he murdered her precisely due to that reason. Without his clarification, she would not have been declared a saint.

Later, he formally requested to live with the Capuchins of the Marches Province. They accepted. The choice to spend the rest of his life in a convent was made due to the humiliations and misunderstandings he encountered in attempting to reintegrate into the world. He was forever known as the murderer of a saint. He was even sometimes accused of crimes just because his name was Alessandro Serenelli. Yet he accepted every hardship as penance in atonement for his sin. Moreover, he also developed a love for silence and solitude, and he wished to live quietly in an oasis of spirituality.

He lived "as a son of St. Francis" in three different Capuchin convents. He went to Mass daily, prayed the office, ate in the same refectory, and slept in a cell. However, he never took vows or became a friar. He remained a layman. He worked as a gardener, porter, and general laborer.

INTRODUCTION

Alessandro Serenelli died on May 6, 1970, at the age of eighty-eight, in the Capuchin infirmary in Macerata. It was the same day and month in which Luigi Goretti had died seventy years earlier.

Those who knew Alessandro said that he died in the peace of Christ, with the love and admiration of many. Among his personal effects, the Capuchin superior found a sealed envelope containing a letter dated May 5, 1961. It was his spiritual testament, an in-depth look into the mystery of a man who had been redeemed and rediscovered his dignity.

1: June 2, 1882

Not far from Ancona is Paterno, a hilltop village overlooking the Adriatic Sea in the region of the Marches. Visitors and locals alike enjoy breathtaking views of the sea to the northeast and the scenic landscapes and mountains in the other direction. Narrow, cobblestone streets wind through the old village, lined with old stone houses, creating an overall charming atmosphere. Though Alessandro Serenelli was born here in 1882, there is no mention of his birth anywhere.

Paterno has a rich history dating back to the medieval era and boasts status as its own municipality. Its elevation of 274 meters (900 ft) rendered it an important part of Ancona's *Castelli* (Castles), that is, Ancona's defensive network during its era as a maritime republic before the unification of Italy. While Paterno was once a thriving municipality, today its resident population has dwindled to just 200 full-time residents. It exists as a *frazione* (hamlet) as part of the metropolitan port city of Ancona. The focal point is the twelfth-century Church of Santa Maria Assunta.

Alessandro Serenelli was born in Paterno, the last of eight children of Cecilia Mangoni and Giovanni Serenelli. He received his name from an older brother born before him who died at the age of two. His birthday, June 2, 1882, is noted in history books as the day "the Hero of the Two Worlds"—that is, Giuseppe Garibaldi—died. Alessandro was baptized the following day in the Church of Santa Maria Assunta.

Alessandro's father, Giovanni Serenelli, was from Loreto (near Ancona). Famed throughout Christendom, since the late thirteenth century, the sanctuary city has safeguarded the walls believed to be part of the Holy House of Mary of Nazareth. Giovanni was born on January 1, 1838, to Piermaria and Angela Serenelli. Cecilia, Alessandro's mother, was born in Montecassiano (near Macerata) in 1845 to Vincenzo Mangoni. Her mother's name is not known. This scant information was obtained from a certificate in the mental hospital in Ancona, where she died.

Giovanni Serenelli's youth and early adulthood seemed promising. His family was well-to-do, and he had an esteemed job working as an estate manager on the lands owned by the Basilica of the Holy House. Sadly, he would experience one tragedy after another, and he would die a ruined man. Alessandro notes the suffering that befell his family.

> I was the last of eight siblings, two of whom died very young. Alessandro, the penultimate, died as a toddler, and his name was then given to me. Vincenzo, whom I did not know, died of scarlet fever at the age of eighteen months. I remember the others: Lucia, Pietro, Enrico, Gaspare, and another Vincenzo, all now deceased. With the exception of the first, all died more or less tragically. Misfortune always raged against my family. [1]

Giovanni's first misfortune took place when he was still in Loreto. Due to his argumentative personality, he began quarreling with relatives over interests. Then he was terminated from his job working for the Basilica of the Holy House. He moved to Paterno, where he found work as a farmhand. He knew how to cultivate grapes, olives, and wheat.

Perhaps her separation from Loreto and her husband's precarious work life led to Alessandro's mother's first breakdown. Cecilia's mental illness and premature death were the first hardships that Alessandro endured. He described it in his memoirs. "My first misfortune in life was that of practically never knowing my mother. She had mental illness and died when I was still a child, so much that I have no memories of her." [2]

The illness was hereditary. Alessandro's brother, Gaspare, also suffered from a form of psychosis.

> At the age of thirteen, my brother Gaspare entered the seminary in Ancona as an adolescent. [...] One day, he was at Adoration before the Blessed Sacrament. The church was deserted, and numerous candles were lit at the altar.

An elderly woman present had an epileptic fit and fell over with her legs in the air. Gaspare was so scared that he returned home, no longer well. He was admitted to a home, but after various alternatives and prolonged hospitalizations, he ended up being admitted to Ancona's psychiatric hospital. 3

Not long after Gaspare was admitted to the asylum in 1885, his mother was admitted. "Out of great disappointment [due to Gaspare's illness], my mother also fell ill and began to do strange things." 4 On June 26, 1885, Cecilia entered the door of the same mental hospital in Ancona after being diagnosed with acute dementia. She was released on November 29. However, she relapsed and returned the following year. She remained in the psychiatric hospital from April 14, 1886, until her death on March 26, 1890. The cause of death was leptomeningitis.

At the time of these tragic events, Alessandro was just a boy. The family illnesses and dynamics would forever mark his personality. On another occasion, he was seriously victimized by his mother during a psychotic episode that took place before her hospitalization. Alessandro's older brother Pietro later told him what happened, since he was a small child and had no memory of it. Alessandro described the horrific event.

Each day, my mother wandered around a well, and every now and then she made the gesture of throwing me into the water. "Mother, what are you doing?" asked Pietro, running up to her in fear. "Poor little thing," replied our mother, referring to me. He will likely have to suffer so much, so it is better that he goes to Heaven now. 5

Despite these tragedies, Alessandro experienced two memorable moments as a child. On August 15, 1888, the Feast of the Assumption, he received the Sacrament of Confirmation. He recalled it nostalgically, remembering the "handsome suit and white shoes" he wore, as well as the gift he received from his godfather of one "scudo"—a large silver coin. 6

Another positive aspect of his childhood was when Alessandro was sent to school at the age of six. Though he received schooling for only about eighteen months, few children whose families worked in agriculture received any education at all. Due to this detail, he was considered the intellectual of the household and beyond, given that literacy was rare in that milieu.

At the beginning of his schooling, he had a kindly teacher whom he described as "good, religious, positive, and affectionate." Her warmth partly filled the void created by the hospitalization and death of his mother. He recalled something she said.

> One day at school, the teacher told us, "The most serious misfortune is the loss of your mother." But I thought to myself, "This is not true! I still have food to eat and clothing, too." Only later did I understand just how true her words were. [7]

Unfortunately, the good teacher fell ill and was replaced by an exceedingly stern man, a veterinarian by trade. He regularly resorted to excessive corporal punishments whenever the slightest discipline issues arose. He would twist the fingers of his pupils until they screamed, strike them with a ruler, or throw a certain ball at their heads. One day, Alessandro was the target of this particular "missile." It bloodied his forehead and left a scar for life.

During this period, Alessandro's sister-in-law, Maria (the wife of his older brother Pietro), sought to look after him and fill the maternal gap that was missing—to the best of her ability. She taught him how to pray and avoid bad influences. Her loving presence was an effort at normality for a boy enduring a period of tremendous sadness. Unfortunately, her good intentions were not enough.

The combination of these hardships was destructive to Alessandro's fragile psyche. He already had a taciturn and introverted character, which was exacerbated by everything he was suffering as a child. Yet his personality now began turning darker. He was submissive to the point of masochism when confronted with those stronger than him, but violent and harsh with those weaker.

---

[1] Fortunato Ciomei, *Il Pugnale dei Tanti Rimorsi* (Nettuno: Santuario Madonna delle Grazie, 1988), 9.
[2] Ibid.
[3] Ibid.

[4] Nadia Tarantini, *Maria Goretti* (Roma: Unità, 1994), 113-4.
[5] Ciomei, *Il Pugnale*, 10.
[6] Ibid., 10.
[7] Ibid.

2: The Sea

In the late nineteenth century, Italy underwent a serious economic depression. The period from 1880 to 1914 resulted in the largest wave of emigration in Italian history. Known as the great Italian diaspora, it is estimated that some 13 to 16 million Italians left their native lands to work elsewhere. This migratory exodus touched one in three families. Italians went north to the industrialized cities of Northern Italy and the Germanic countries, while others left for the Americas. Many families from the Marches region headed to the large agricultural estates in the Roman countryside, to the east and south of Rome. This would be the eventual choice of the Serenelli and Goretti families.

But for now, Giovanni Serenelli sought out a closer destination. After the death of his wife, Giovanni left Paterno and relocated with his family to nearby Torrette, a small village on the sea just ten kilometers (6 mi) from Paterno. At fifty-six years old, Giovanni had grown tired of the backbreaking labor in the fields, and he sought out less physical work.

When Alessandro and his family arrived in Torrette, in the late nineteenth century, Torrette was a small, seaside village nestled on the outskirts of Ancona. "In my time, there was only a tavern and a few houses along the railway." [8] Most residents worked at the docks or out at sea. In the parish archives of the Church of Maria Santissima Madre di Dio (Mary Most Holy Mother of God), located on Via Metauro in Torrette, there is a record of the arrival of the Serenelli family. It states that the family moved to Torrette from Paterno in 1894 and settled in a rented house belonging to a gentleman named Giambattista Baldinelli in the Marina 21 district.

Since Giovanni already had a horse, he bought a cart and began transporting goods and passengers from the nearby port of Ancona to Rome and other destinations. It was a busy life, focused on making ends meet. However, in the process, he neglected the upbringing of the youngest children, including Alessandro. By necessity, he was entrusted to the care of friends and relatives. Among his travels back and forth to the capital city of Italy, instead of acquiring financial success, he picked up malaria. His poor health led poor Giovanni to turn to the bottle, an important detail that would affect his relationships with those around him.

Since childhood, Alessandro had always been enamored by the sea. From the hilltop position of Paterno, he had a beautiful view of the promontory, known as Mount Conero, just south of Ancona. With its enigmatic white cliffs jutting straight into the sea, it was an impressive site. It appeared like a blade, cutting through the fog and clouds. Alessandro once described his fascination with the sea.

> From my school window [in Paterno], I looked into the distance and saw the vast, blue sea, as well as boats sailing among the waves. I remember thinking to myself how beautiful it would be to go to the sea, so far away. I dreamed of being happy. [9]

Alessandro spent the early period in Torrette, living with his brother Pietro and his wife, Maria Gatti. She was born on January 16, 1869, in Ancona. As alluded to earlier, Maria was one of the most positive role models in Alessandro's adolescence. She took his fate to heart, striving to teach him right from wrong with a firm hand. Alessandro said that "Maria often scolded me because I hung out with bad friends on the street—all sons of fishermen." [10]

At twelve years old, in the parish of Madre di Dio (Mother of God), Alessandro received his First Communion. [Editor: In the past, the faithful received Confirmation before Communion.] It was arranged by his sister-in-law, Maria, and the parish priest. Alessandro noted that it was a "beautiful day." [11] Sadly, we rarely come across that word when reconstructing his life. In fact, when Alessandro further described that day, he said that "the parish priest was a good man, but I was a shameful fellow, because I was accustomed to the countryside." [12] The word shame seems to better qualify many aspects of his youth—especially his character.

While Alessandro had attended school in Paterno and knew how to read and write, after the family's move to Torrette, virtually all his companions and their fathers were illiterate sailors. Given that Giovanni was away frequently, Alessandro decided to go to work at sea. When his brother Pietro—who was working on a flat-bottomed boat—suggested he join him, twelve-year-old Alessandro did not hesitate.

> With that, I began life at sea, where I was employed for almost five years. I stayed in the water, but I never learned to swim due to my shy and reserved nature. I spent the first months working on flat-bottomed boats with Pietro. Then I found a better employer, a gentleman named Gilberto Ferretti, who regularly paid the sailors. He gave me ten lire a week. [13]

The boats would set out early in the morning or in the evening for longer voyages. Sailboats were used to transport stones, coal, and gravel to the mercantile ports of Senigallia, Fano, Pesaro, and Porto Recanati. For the adolescents who worked on these ships, the conditions were unsafe. This was well before the social welfare laws that were enacted in Italy, predominantly after World War II. Instead, the boys who worked at sea had many responsibilities and few rights. They were often exploited by unscrupulous men who forced them to work in precarious conditions. In such a context, the moral environment was bad.

After a few months, following the suggestion of his brother Pietro and enticed by a better salary, Alessandro left his job on the flat-bottomed boat to become a fisherman. Embarkment took place at dusk, fishing lasted throughout the night, and the return was at sunrise. During the day, there was much to do. At the docks, the boys mended nets, lined up boxes, and prepared the oil lamps. The fishing work was frenetic: they lowered the nets, drew them back in, and had to learn to move in coordination among the waves and sea currents. The nets were described as "puffy-headed," that is, equipped with lead for deep-water fishing. Otherwise, they used a net called a "devil-chaser" for fishing on the surface.

Alessandro had vivid memories of his work at sea.

> The most prized fish was sea bass. It sold for sixty cents a kilogram, compared to other fish, which went for less than

> thirty. When you went offshore, you had to watch out for the dolphins. Big and black, they would dive in the water, and they were always very hungry. When they heard the boats, they would swim up to them and run their noses along the rope until they got to the net bag and had a snack. We cabin boys were in charge of chasing them away by making noise on the wood of the boat. They would always flee in fear at the noise. [14]

Alessandro worked at sea for three years, a period he recalled with ambiguity. On the one hand, he was drawn to the sea. At the same time, he was scared of the water. He said, "I didn't like the [sea] profession, so much so that I never wanted to learn how to swim. The water scared me and at the same time attracted me." [15]

Alessandro also identified that period as the origin of his going astray. He described what it was like.

> The environment at sea was not the most suitable for a healthy upbringing. In addition to [sailors'] constant blasphemies, they regarded the Church very little. They would send their wives and children to church and go there to get married or for some other event. [My sister-in-law] Maria encouraged me to go to church, but Ancona had a reputation for being subversive. The people didn't like priests or the government. [16]

During this period, Pietro and Maria were becoming increasingly distant. In their place, Alessandro was being formed by the unsavory characters and personages he spent most of his time with—dissolute adolescents and unscrupulous adults at the docks and at sea. And yet, despite all the precariousness, Alessandro recalls the presence of God and how he experienced God's omnipotence and providence in his life.

> God never abandoned me. I will never forget an event that reveals his providential protection toward me. [...] My father was headed toward Rome. Before he left, I went to say goodbye to him at the Falconara train station, so I couldn't go to sea that day. That day, there was a storm, and the large boat I was supposed to work on capsized. The sailors were thrown violently into the water, and they barely reached land. When they called the roll, the boy who

took my place, who was my friend and the same age as me, didn't answer. He had been below deck, and he drowned. The sea was his grave. I will never forget the scene of his desolate mother, who cried out to her son. The poor woman had given him a hard-boiled egg that morning to encourage him to go on board. He was afraid of the water, but he obeyed his mother's will. I still have that woman's cries in my memory. But just think that I was supposed to go out to sea! God saved me. May God be blessed! Despite that memory, I have always had a great love for the sea. The breath of the sea breeze opens my heart and fills the emptiness inside; it fills the need for affection that I never had. [17]

While it is natural to question the logic of a God who would allow one boy to die so that another would be saved—and how history might have been different had it been Alessandro who drowned that day—one thing is certain: God loves all people, and he always provides for all in every circumstance. For we "know that all things work for good for those who love God, who are called according to his purpose" (Romans 8:28).

---

[8] Ciomei, *Il Pugnale*, 11.
[9] Ibid.
[10] Ibid., 10.
[11] Ibid., 11.
[12] Ibid.
[13] Ibid., 12.
[14] Ibid.
[15] Ibid., 13.
[16] Ibid., 12.
[17] Ibid., 13.

3: Toward the Roman Countryside

Within one year of one another, two men and their families boarded the same train line from Falconara to Rome. Like so many other migrants, Luigi Goretti and Giovanni Serenelli hoped for a better future for themselves and their families. Saddled with trunks, boxes, and bundles, they said their *Addio* to family and friends, as well as to the land that some of them would never see again. Though Luigi and Giovanni didn't know one another, their destinies would soon become intertwined. In circumstances both terrible and glorious, their names were about to enter the annals of history.

In autumn 1895, Giovanni Serenelli decided to sever ties with his native region of the Marches and head south to work in the countryside outside of Rome. With him were two sons, Gaspare and Vincenzo, while Pietro and Lucia stayed behind in Torrette. Alessandro, then thirteen years old, continued to live with Pietro and Maria.

A little over one year later, on December 12, 1896, the same fate befell Luigi Goretti. After the harvest, Luigi's sharecropping contract in Corinaldo was terminated, and he had no choice but to emigrate. The land in Corinaldo had not been generous to him. Luigi was headed to the Colle Gianturco hamlet near Paliano in the Roman countryside. With him were his wife Assunta and their four children: Angelo, Alessandro, Mariano, and little Maria.

When the Goretti family set out, Giovanni and his two sons had been in Olevano Romano, not far from Paliano, for a little over a year. In one of his numerous journeys as a courier down to Rome, Giovanni met a landowner named Cappellini. The arrival of the Serenelli father and sons was recorded in the Olevano municipal register on October 22, 1895. Also recorded was the address of their dwelling: Contrada Collecardo Vigna Cappellini.

Cappellini was a wealthy Protestant pastor, and he owned a large estate on the Colle Cardo hillside near Olevano. He was looking for laborers and was fond of workers from the Marches region. In addition to offering free housing, he also paid for his tenants' travel expenses.

The terrain that the Serenelli men were hired to work on was not the best. The land was rugged and steep, though partially terraced. The south-facing hill was very hot in summer and cold in early winter, during the olive harvest, which they discovered just after they arrived. Another problem revealed itself later. When they arrived, Cappellini told them, "In the beginning, you will work with farm tools. Later, you will have animals, as is customary among you from the Marches." [18] But the animals never arrived.

The people of the Marches were generally optimistic. However, as the months passed, it became clear that the work was more grueling than Serenelli had anticipated. The transition from working the gentle hills of the Marches region, where work was carried out with animals, to the steep terrain of Colle Cardo, where everything was done with spades and hoes, was difficult. On various occasions, Giovanni asked Cappellini about the animals, to which he insisted they were on the way.

There were other setbacks. Since his first admission to the mental hospital in Ancona, Gaspare Serenelli had never been in great health. In Olevano, he became ill again. Sadly, he would return to the psychiatric ward, first in Rome and later in Ancona again. Then, Giovanni's other son, Vincenzo, was conscripted to serve in the military, as three years of military service were compulsory in Italy during that period. With his two sons no longer available to work with him in the fields and considering the contract he had with Cappellini, Giovanni sent a letter to Alessandro, in which he asked him to join him in Olevano. His youngest son agreed.

[18] Ciomei, *Il Pugnale*, 14.

4: Alessandro's Arrival

In summer 1897, the final protagonist set out on the Falconara-Rome rail line. Alessandro was content to leave Torrette. He had qualms about the life of a fisherman. The environment was rife with vulgarity and depravity. Alessandro said, "When I was a sailor's assistant in Torrette, unfortunately, I associated with licentious companions. Therefore, my soul became corrupt, a fact that persisted, or rather, became accentuated in the countryside. By nature, I was, instead, a lover of solitude." [19]

The journey to the Roman countryside was a festive affair for the fifteen-year-old Serenelli boy. Since he was a minor, one of Cappellini's assistants journeyed from Rome all the way to Ancona to pick him up and accompany him back. When they arrived in Rome, he gave him a tour of the Eternal City. For an adolescent who had spent his life among the countryside of Paterno and the sea of Torrette, one can only imagine how he would have been struck by the sights of the Eternal City. Alessandro recalled his visit. "He took me to see St. Peter's Basilica, the fountains, and the Tiber River." [20]

Alessandro's arrival in Olevano was recorded in the municipal register on June 20, 1897, his residence recorded at Vigna Cappellini. When he arrived, he was overjoyed. Not only was he reunited with his father after almost two years, he would also be working the land, for which he had an innate love. Working on the land would be healthier—morally as well as physically—than working at sea. Farmers were simple people, but they were earthy and practical. He had arrived just in time for the summer harvest. The scythes were sharpened and put to the fields, swaying with heavy, golden wheat.

Though the environment was better for Alessandro, there were challenges. By now, Giovanni was acquainted with the personality of the owner of the Colle Cardo estate. Cappellini's bizarre and, at times, erratic behavior became clear. He preferred to be called Protestant Bishop by the townspeople and his hired hands alike, although he was probably just an evangelical pastor. Surely, he was a good entrepreneur with a knack for proselytism. He took his farmhands to "his church," in which he officiated with great oratorical skills. His wife also lived on the estate. She was known as a "priest-eater" and was a staunch enemy of the pope. She gave Alessandro the Book of Esther, which he never read. He never "converted."

Religious sensibilities aside, Mr. Cappellini managed his estate in an overbearing manner. Each year, he gave his workers a barrel of new wine, but he also demanded that they remove their hats when he passed. One day, Giovanni Serenelli's temper flared. "As my landlord, I respect you, but as for the rest, we know how to behave!" [21]

In Olevano, Alessandro met the Passionist priests for the first time. The order (technically, a congregation) was founded by St. Paul of the Cross in 1700, with a mission toward evangelization and a particular charism of commemorating the Passion of Jesus. The Passionists were (and still are) widespread in the countryside around Rome. They would play a key role in the period before and after Maria Goretti's canonization.

In preparation for the Holy Year of 1900, the Passionists held a mission in Olevano. Despite Cappellini's and his wife's strong opposition, the Olevano mission was an overwhelming success. "I went to listen to the Fathers' sermons," Alessandro recalled, "and was struck by young people who gave up their daggers, sticking them into a piece of wood at the altar of the Virgin." [22] After years of indifference toward religion, Serenelli had a change of heart during this period. It was a period of spiritual sensitivity after an adolescence marked by difficulties and confusion. The seeds of grace were beginning to root. Tragically, the darkness would return—in all its wickedness.

Meanwhile, Giovanni Serenelli was becoming more and more

unhappy with working conditions at Colle Cardo. Noted for his proud character, he began to resent his lot in life. He, who had once been an estate manager in Loreto, was now a sharecropper migrant. When he realized that the promised beasts of burden were never coming, he had had enough. It was the proverbial straw that broke the camel's back.

Alessandro recalled the clash between his father and Cappellini. "One day, my father went to the owner and said to him, 'We work like beasts, but we are not beasts. We will no longer work under these conditions.'" [23] Struck by Serenelli's curtness, Cappellini didn't respond. Instead, he fired the father-and-son team on the spot. They had to leave.

Who knows what went through Alessandro's mind in that moment? His response is not recorded anywhere. Was he disappointed in his father? Did he perceive this latest plight as another confirmation that he was destined to fail? Or was he too preoccupied with where he would go next to think of these things?

Fortunately, it didn't take long for Giovanni to find work. In October 1989, he and his son found another sharecropping stint on a farm near Paliano, some ten kilometers (6 mi) from Olevano. They would be working on an estate owned by a Roman senator named Scelsi. The site, in Colle Gianturco, is of utmost significance. Here, they would meet Luigi Goretti and his children, including Maria. No one could have ever imagined what would take place.

---

[19] Proc. Inf., 166-167.
[20] Ciomei, *Il Pugnale*, 14.
[21] Ciomei, *Il Pugnale*, 15.
[22] Ibid.
[23] Ibid.

5: The Meeting of the Serenellis and Gorettis

The Goretti family arrived in Colle Gianturco on December 13, 1896, the Feast of St. Lucia, as noted in the municipal register of Paliano. [24] Accompanying Luigi were his twenty-six-year-old wife Assunta and his children Angelo, Alessandro, Mariano, and Marietta. His brother, Sante, had also come with his family.

Luigi was mild-mannered, positive, and industrious. He immediately found a good work-life balance in his new home. On Sundays, he and his family attended the Passionist church of Santa Maria di Pugliano. Luigi had a glimmer of hope that they could build a better future. His brother, Sante, however, had other ideas. On August 7, 1897, not long after they arrived, Sante decided to return home to Corinaldo. His decision was a crushing blow for Luigi. However, he would make the best of the situation.

When Giovanni Serenelli arrived in Colle Gianturco in late 1898 with Alessandro, the harvest was not yet completed. Giovanni was sixty years old and in bad health due to malaria and wine. Senator Scelsi—ever reasonable and diplomatic—had an idea. He devised a plan that would appeal to the heads of both families. Life in the countryside was difficult for anyone, yet more so for Luigi, as he had a large family to feed. Now that his brother had left, he needed to work with another man. For the Serenellis, who were without a wife and mother, a partnership with a good family could offer a sense of warmth. A collaboration seemed like a good idea to Luigi, as well as to the Serenellis. They all agreed.

In the beginning, Alessandro came across as an ordinary adolescent, if not introverted. Assunta Goretti later described how she perceived the sixteen-year-old Alessandro when they met.

> He was a physically well-developed and robust young man, assiduous at work, and respectful towards his father and me. Every Sunday he came to Mass, every two months he received the sacraments, and he said the Rosary with us every evening. However, he was of a closed, solitary, and cold nature, and he avoided the company of others. When he wasn't working, he closed himself in his room, absorbed, I believe, in his readings. [25]

In all honesty, Luigi and Assunta should have been more prudent in discerning Scelsi's proposal. While it was practically advantageous, there were real risks. The reality is that the agreement stipulated that not only would they work together, they would share the same house. The two families would live under the same roof and share meals together, as if they were an extended family. It didn't take long for Luigi to realize that Giovanni Serenelli was overbearing. Accustomed to his past position as a foreman, he quickly proclaimed himself head of the two families and decided that he would be the point of contact regarding relations with the landlord.

Indeed, not long after they began working together, the difficulties became apparent. This is how Alessandro described their situation in Colle Gianturco.

> Beginning that year, Scelsi gave his lands to sharecroppers, while previously he had worked with his own teams of employees called "corporals." In Colle Gianturco, there were animals; they didn't have only hoes like in Olevano. However, the soil was poor, and little grew; there was poor wheat and corn only if it rained. The sharecroppers said that it was bad in Corinaldo but worse here. The managers treated their employees poorly. The head of management was the son of Senator Giuseppe Scelsi, named Messor Peppino. And he was keen to be called by this name. If any one of us, unaware, called him Messor Giuseppe, he would immediately scold him, saying, "I'm not Messor Giuseppe but Messor Peppino, and that's how it is!" [26]

Given the situation, it is not difficult to imagine how a clash between Giovanni Serenelli and Messor Peppino was inevitable.

The passive Luigi Goretti, true to his character, stayed quiet. Alessandro recalls the moment:
> My father, given the poor conditions in which we found ourselves and recalling that he had once been an estate manager, perhaps thought of our old proverb that says, "When you have been an estate manager for a year, if you don't get rich, it's to your detriment." After four months, he had a disagreement with the boss. In February 1899, my father had a major blowout with Messor Peppino. I'm not sure exactly what the reason was, though it was certainly due to working conditions. The fact is that [my father] blew up at the landlord, who immediately fired my father and the Goretti family, who were working associates with him. [27]

The break was not only due to working conditions. Intolerant of any authority, proud and ever-obstinate, the elder Serenelli had already been looking for better land. He had come into contact with a nobleman named Count Attilio Mazzoleni—also known as "the Roman merchant"—who owned a large estate in a town called Conca near Le Ferriere. The sensitive Messor Peppino, having discovered the scheming, summoned both Serenelli and Goretti and fired them on the spot. Another door was closed for Giovanni Serenelli. This time, Luigi Goretti and his family were sucked in.

Assunta recalled simply that the "land in Colle Gianturco was not profitable because it needed to be reclaimed. The entire time we were there, we had only corn bread and polenta to eat." [28] It was February 1899 when the two families set out yet again. This time, no one—except perhaps Giovanni Serenelli—was enthusiastic about the future. They were headed into the swamps.

---

[24] Book of Residents of the Municipality of Paliano.
[25] Mauro Liberati. *Maria Goretti*. (Roma: Coletti, II. Ed., 1960), 64.
[26] Ciomei, *Il Pugnale*, 17.
[27] Ibid.
[28] Document in envelope, no. 3.

6: The Pontine Marshes

Ever convinced that "God always provides," good Luigi set out once again. Count Attilio Mazzoleni formally invited the two families to work for him.

> Come down immediately. Up there, you eat polenta and cornbread. At my place, you will have bread made from real wheat, live in a brick house, which is rare in these places, and have a sharecropping contract. You [the Serenelli and Goretti families] can continue to work together because the house is large and the land consists of about twenty hectares. [29]

With that, they dusted off the old boxes, tied up the blankets and work tools, closed the door, and set out again, this time by carriage to the railway station. The Gorettis huddled together among bumps and potholes as they traveled thirty kilometers toward the heart of the Planet of Mosquitoes. It was dark and cold. They got off at Cecchina, where two carters, sent by Mazzoleni, were waiting for them. It was a memorable journey that remained forever impressed in Alessandro's mind.

> In that period, the countryside was all frosty because it was still winter. We passed through Valmontone, Artena, Lariano, and Velletri up to Cecchina. In two carriages, driven by two of Mazzoleni's carters, we set off at a horse's pace. At Osteriaccia, now Campoleone, we left Via Nettunense and took Via Torre Spaccasassi. Then we passed Carano and Campomorto on our way down to Le Ferriere. [30]

Shortly after the Astura River, the silhouettes of two farmhouses came into view. It was the end of a long odyssey, especially for the Goretti children. By now, it was the middle of the night. In the distance, they could hear the rustling of the river and the croaking of frogs. By torchlight, they were greeted by the Cimarelli family, also from Corinaldo, who had prepared dinner. Their kind gesture was like a caress of God—familial warmth despite the coldness all around them.

There is no record of the arrival of Giovanni Serenelli and Luigi Goretti or their families in the municipal or parish registers during the month of February 1899. Perhaps it was their destiny to remain anonymous. And yet what would soon happen in the Pontine Marshes would reverberate throughout the region, the country, and the world.

The Pontine Marshes were a vast, low-lying wetland area beginning along the coast of the Tyrrhenian Sea southeast of Rome, roughly between Anzio and Terracina, and bordered by the Volscian Mountains to the east. The region consisted of a mix of forested grasslands above sea level and mud flats and stagnant ponds below. The area was prone to flooding and remained largely uninhabited due to the prevalence of malaria. Today, they no longer exist. They were drained during the reign of Mussolini in the early twentieth century.

The Marshes are linked with infamy. Vintage photos depict a monotonous and lifeless landscape made up of brushwood and stagnant ponds, while herds of horses, buffalo, and sheep roam the countryside. The inhabitants of the Pontine Marshes had a bad reputation. Many were descendants of convicts and thieves who sought refuge in this land, where it was easy to hide.

What made life more precarious was malaria. It is said that passengers traveling by train south of Terracina had to be prepared. The conductor would pass by to tell the passengers to close the window tightly and cover their mouths and noses with a kerchief. This was to guard against the foul-smelling *miasma* (bad air) that would soon fill the carriages. Passengers who dared look out the window would see a gray sky filled with angry swarms of insects. Rows of animal carcasses made it appear that the entire area was cursed.

One century earlier, the German poet Goethe wrote that this entire region was inhabited by "savages afflicted with the fever," that is, malaria. This was the great curse of the marshes. It was so widespread that the locals had a name for it in their dialect: *commare*. Long dreaded since ancient times, malaria was described by the ancient Roman writer Pliny. In the early 1900s, the sick were still treated with primitive remedies.

The cause of the disease had colorful explanations. Sometimes the humidity was blamed, while other times it was the fault of uncultivated fields. Some believed malaria was due to the humid winds, the hot temperatures, or the rotting herbs. Or perhaps it was caused by the mixing of salt water and fresh water. Whatever the cause, all were convinced that the disease was due to "bad air"—hence its name, "malaria."

By 1900, it was discovered that the actual culprit of the disease was anopheles (a mosquito species) and that quinine—a white crystalline alkaloid—could be used to treat it. But prejudices and superstition ran deep. Unfortunately, doctors were limited by miserly landlords who didn't want to offer care for their tenants. Landlords of the estates not only opposed the diagnosis of malaria, they discouraged doctors from entering the territory, rendering their work useless and unappreciated.

Despite the hardships, there were moments of fun in the swamps. For several days, the monotony of peasant life was replaced by games, entertainment, and revelry for the annual festival, known as the *merca*, when cattle were branded. The noblemen of the Roman aristocracy would show up for what was a veritable rootin'-tootin' rodeo. While the aristocratic men participated in hunts of pheasants, rabbits, pigeons, and foxes, the noble women pranced around in their Victorian-era elaborate dresses, made of rich silks, velvets, and brocades, and their elaborate hats and hairstyles, adorned with feathers, ribbons, and jewels. They stood in sharp contrast with the peasant women of the marshes, who wore long wool skirts, aprons, and sturdy boots, their heads covered in plain kerchiefs.

Given the precarious working and living conditions, only the desperate came into the Pontine Marshes to work. At the turn of the century, thousands of peasants came from the Marches and Abruzzo regions for the nine-month season from September through June. They were sharecroppers. The landlords—usually

Roman nobility—would lease their land to the farmers, who would have to pay somewhere between 30% and 50% of the yield in crops to the owner.

On a typical plot of land, after years of working for the landlord, an average family would be forced to take on debts for seed, farm tools, and loans. There was often no way to repay the money and get out of debt, not least because many were sickened or killed from malaria. Overcome by desperation and hunger, they would often be forced to leave the fields and set out on another painful migration. This was the environment the Goretti and Serenelli families had descended into.

---

[29] Ciomei, *Il Pugnale*, 19.
[30] Ibid.

7: The Cascina Antica

Along State Highway 148, at marker km 58, a directional arrow points toward the town of Le Ferriere to the right. A slight street—vibrant and luminous—winds among villas and farmhouses. Today, the farmland yields grapes and cereals, while greenhouses are utilized for more serious cultivation. The panorama is immensely serene. In the center of town is an old smokestack—all that remains of the old paper mill. Across the street is another small hamlet with a church dedicated to St. Anthony. Other than that, there is only a newsstand, a butcher shop, and a bridge over the Astura River.

Just beyond the river are three large, restored farmhouses. These are the last witnesses to the tragedy that still feels palpable. From a distance, one can hear the voices of children playing in the yard in front of the farmhouse. While it was once the scene of an awful tragedy, today it has been converted into a preschool run by Passionist sisters.

A few kilometers away is the village of Borgo Montello, formerly known as Conca. The warehouses and palace that once belonged to Mazzoleni have also been restored and serve as municipal buildings. Nearby is the parish church dedicated to the Annunciation, where Marietta received her First Communion.

This land boasts a rich history. Le Ferriere is the site of the ancient city of Satricum. Pre-dating the Roman era, archaeological evidence suggests Satricum dates as far back as the ninth century B.C. By the sixth century, it had developed into a prosperous urban center. Satricum was involved in the wars between the Romans, Volsci, Latins, and Ernili for control of the Italian peninsula. Its end came suddenly when the Romans conquered it in 385 B.C. and razed it to the ground. Today, all that remains of Satricum is a museum, housing numerous ancient artifacts.

The name, Le Ferriere, is relatively recent. It derives from an important iron mill developed under Pope Sixtus V around the year 1589. [Editor: The Italian word for iron is *ferro*.] The steel industry was thriving then, and iron developed here was used in construction throughout the Grand Duchy of Tuscany as well as in the Kingdom of Naples. Later, during restoration to the dome of St. Peter's carried out in the eighteenth century, the iron work came from "the renowned Ferriere of Conca." [31]

The farmhouse where the Goretti and Serenelli families lived is referred to as the Cascina Antica, or the Ancient Farmhouse. To its left is another one, where the Cimarelli brothers (Mario, Domenico, and Angelo) lived with their families. The Cimarellis were also from Corinaldo, and the friendship that consolidated over time would enter significantly into the story we are telling. Mario's wife, Teresa, was Marietta's close friend. Together with her husband, she played an important role in the dramatic moments on July 5, 1902.

When Luigi and Giovanni arrived at the Cascina Antica, they climbed the steep staircase up into the large kitchen. The Serenelli father and son took the rooms on the right, while the Gorettis took the rooms on the left. The large kitchen separated the living quarters. Alessandro described the arrival:

> Marietta, then nine years old, served dinner. I noticed her candor and innate goodness. God gave me a little sister, and my closed and grumpy character had the opportunity to open up before the goodness and kindness that came from that little girl. Marietta was shy and reserved, especially in the presence of strangers. Later, she would consider me an older brother, showing me a sincere and pure affection that I betrayed on that awful day. After dinner, we recited the Holy Rosary. We Serenelli men joined this practice without difficulty; we were not accustomed to it, but we never abandoned it. Later that night, after making a makeshift bed with a bit of straw, we went to bed very tired. [32]

The next day, the two families met the owner of the house and land, Count Attilio Mazzoleni. Referred to as the "Monarch of the

Swamps," he was exceedingly wealthy. His vast patrimony consisted of 9,800 hectares (24,200 acres) of land in and around Conca; 5,000 sheep, oxen, and horses; houses in Rome; and a baronial palace in Conca. Though he was referred to as a count, he was actually from the middle class. He received his noble title through marriage when he married the Roman noblewoman, Lady Maria Bruschi Falgari. Upon their engagement, he gifted her with a pearl necklace. It cost 250,000 lire, the equivalent of 350 years of labor of a sharecropper on one of his estates.

Mazzoleni rented the two families twenty hectares (50 acres). His policy was to take a third of the harvest if he rented the land. If he contributed to the costs of planting and harvesting, he would take half. The latter was the case of the two newly arrived families. Making matters worse, it was awful land, and only the dry parts were cultivable.

Mazzoleni had an authoritarian character and was sharp with his tenants. He was also anticlerical. "He harassed us incredibly," Alessandro later said. "He continually mistreated us." [33] The day before Marietta's death, Count Mazzoleni went to the threshing floor, where the beans were about to be threshed. He promised that if he found "even one bean among the waste, he would take one additional quintal as punishment." [34]

When Luigi Goretti was ill with malaria, the count sent a bottle of Marsala wine. The old remedy was to "sweat it out." He could have sent quinine, which hadn't yet become customary in the swamps. A law would soon be passed by the Italian parliament making it obligatory. This may have saved his life.

The count's fame lives on due to the daughter of poor Luigi Goretti. Marietta came to his house to learn catechism. He probably never noticed her, as he was preoccupied with his businesses and his sharecroppers, cattlemen, mowers, and seasonal workers. He saw her placed on a stretcher on that tragic July 5, 1902, and even attended her funeral. Despite everything, when Count Mazzoleni returned to Conca after Marietta's funeral in Nettuno, he evicted Giovanni Serenelli, Assunta and her children, and the Cimarellis. He wanted to rid himself of the negative publicity that had been generated by the murder.

There are old black-and-white photographs, yellowed with age, of the Monarch of the Swamp. He rides on horseback with one hand in his pocket, a haughty mien, and a whip over his wrist. He has the air of someone who has the world at his beck and call. He did. Today, however, of his immense patrimony, nothing is left. The only witnesses to his former splendor are the renovated warehouses on the hill of Conca (now Borgo Montello) and the Cascina Antica. He died when his empire was crumbling.

---

[31] Nicola Nicolai, *Atti dell'Accademia Romana d'Archeologia-Storia dei luoghi una volta abitati dell'Agro Romano*, 1828.
[32] Tomás Pujadas, *Yo maté a Maria Goretti*, (Madrid: 1962). 46.
[33] Proc. Inf., 123-4.
[34] Giordano Bruno Guerri, *Povera santa, povero assassino*, (Milan: Mondadori, 1985), 109.

8: The Death of Luigi Goretti

After arriving in Conca, life initially went well for Luigi and Giovanni. Alessandro recalls the period after they arrived in Conca.
> When we arrived, we sowed. The wheat yielded us ten to one the sowing, while in all the other places, it yielded triple and quadruple. We sowed seven quintals of wheat, and in just over three months, we harvested over seventy quintals. The following year, the harvest was around 200 quintals. There were also several quintals of fava beans and fodder for livestock. [Editor: One quintal = 220 lbs.] There was serenity between our two families. The bread we ate was good. It was made from wheat, instead of corn. [35]

The men spent their days entirely occupied with work in the fields. The twenty hectares did not allow for much idle time. During the winter, in the spacious stable located on the ground floor, there was the task of making baskets, stuffing chairs, arranging ladders, and sharpening the agricultural tools, such as spades and scythes. Work went from dawn to dusk.

In addition to all this, there were the animals and housework to tend to, plus keeping in touch with Mazzoleni. Assunta looked after the housework and, with Angelo, looked after the vegetable garden and the larger animals. Maria took care of her younger siblings, tidied up the house, and fed the chickens and pigeons.

The contract was signed by Giovanni Serenelli, to whom the good Luigi had delegated powers of representation. His naive trust would come back to haunt him. Meanwhile, as cohabitation between the two families wore on, differences began to surface, especially as regards mentality and habits. Luigi, however, was always tolerant, a trait he had to lean on heavily in order to live amicably with the temperamental Serenelli father and son. All in all, it appeared that things were normal.

As a confirmation that all was well, Teresa, the last child born to the Gorettis, came into this world on February 2, 1900. The baptism took place in the church of St. Anthony, and Mario Cimarelli and his wife Teresa stood in as godparents. It was a day of great joy, which was also shared with the Serenellis. However, a few days later, the first tragedy struck. Luigi's symptoms began to manifest in early March.

The first symptom was an unusual malaise. Luigi felt excessively tired and lost his appetite. Assunta told him that it was probably due to "the change of season," and everything would pass quickly. She was absorbed in looking after her infant and did not pay heed to Luigi's ailments. Moreover, the Serenellis would not consider slowing the pace of their field work now that the season was just getting underway.

However, Luigi felt his strength slip away further. He felt cold deep in his bones. When he became feverish, they called Mazzoleni, who summoned Dr. Augusto Maggi, who was assigned to the marshes. His diagnosis could not have been worse. Luigi had malaria, meningitis, and pneumonia. Luigi's agony lasted ten days. During that period, Marietta went to Conca, some two kilometers (1.3 mi) away, to get medicine. Together with her siblings, they prayed together for their father. Sensing the seriousness of his condition, Luigi told Assunta several times that she should return to Corinaldo.

Luigi died on May 6, 1900. The chaplain in Conca during that period was Fr. Alfredo Paliani, a Passionist priest. He assisted Luigi in his final moments and presided over the funeral Mass and Luigi's interment in the small cemetery of Conca. Alessandro recalled the funeral, "He was accompanied to the cemetery not with the usual stretcher but with the Goretti family's cart and oxen. I drove the animals during the sad procession, while Angelo, Luigi's son, held the coffin on the cart." [36]

During this period of mourning, the first words of St. Maria Goretti to her mother were as follows, "Mamma, do not be discouraged. You can take Papa's place in the field work, and I will look after the household duties. God will not abandon us. You will see. We will get by." [37] This was a promise to which Marietta would always remain faithful. It reveals the degree of her human and spiritual maturity. Mamma Assunta confirmed her sincerity.

> Marietta was there for the housework, and then I would arrive at the last moment to lend her a hand. She corrected the little siblings, and when the eldest gave me some displeasure, she scolded him, saying, "You do this because your father is no longer here. He had a generous heart towards me and towards our siblings; in eating, he pleased others first, then himself." [38]

At the end of the year, despite the good harvest of 300 quintals of wheat and ninety-six quintals of field beans, after squaring accounts with Mazzoleni, Assunta and Giovanni still owed fifteen lire. This was the second misfortune in Conca that year. The third and worst tragedy was about to take place.

---

[35] Ciomei, *Il Pugnale*, 21.
[36] Ibid., 21-22.
[37] Giovanni Alberti, *Maria Goretti*, (Nettuno: Santuario Madonna delle Grazie: IV ed., 2003), 139.
[38] Acts of the Apostolic Process, 238.

9: How I Remember Her

Alessandro said that Maria was always "good, obedient, devoted, and serious. She was not light-hearted or fickle like other little girls. She was happy with whatever clothes her mother made for her or some woman gave her." [39]

He described her more thoroughly.

> I met Maria Goretti and lived in the same farmhouse on the estate of Mr. Scelsi of Paliano and later on the estate owned by Attilio Mazzoleni in Conca. I practically lived with her from 1899 to 1902, when "the deed" took place. She received an education from her parents, especially her mother. Her godmother, Teresa Cimarelli, and the maid of the owner of the estate must also have contributed to her education. She was educated in the rudiments of religion, and many times, following her mother's suggestions, I saw her teach her brothers prayers. Every evening, [the Goretti family] said the Rosary in common, and I also took part. Following in her mother's footsteps, she was modest. She wore long dresses, and she never uncovered herself, even in the hot summertime. I remember in particular that there were certain girls from a family who lived near our house, whose company Maria fled because they were a bit licentious. She drew water quickly, so much so that we marveled at how fast she came home. When she went on errands, she went straight on her way. Even when dealing with her younger brothers, I always observed her to be very modest. I had newspapers and illustrated periodicals, and I noticed that she never stopped to browse or look at certain illustrations. I had a lot of respect for her, due to

how proper she was. [...] She always went to Mass willingly and even, at times, when it required two hours of walking. The Holy Rosary was said every evening, especially in winter. I deduce that she had a special devotion to Our Lady from the fact that I saw her at Mass and often at home with the Rosary in her hand. At home, she also decorated the image of Our Lady with flowers. She also had devotion to other saints, such as the patron saint of her hometown [St. Anne], and to the souls in Purgatory. After her father's death, she made suffrages for his soul in particular. She offered her First Communion for him. Maria had ordinary features and did not attract attention to herself: blonde hair knotted at the nape of the neck, brown eyes, and a full face. For her age, she was developed, but not as much as they described or represented. She arrived at my shoulders, and I'm not tall; I measure 162 centimeters (5'4"). After all, her parents, sisters, and brothers are all a little short in height, and they all look a little like "water drops." She parted her hair in the middle, was always very modest in everything, and she did everything herself. When Assunta wasn't there, she ran the house. She wore a skirt in not-too-light colors, with a colored kerchief knotted around her neck. However, on the day of my crime, she was wearing a two-piece dress, a skirt, and a red-striped bust given to her by Assunta Casoni, a young lady now getting on in years, who lived near the church of St. Anthony. The artists tried to represent her features. They went by deduction because, in those days, photographs were rare, and we didn't even think about [having one made]. In my humble opinion, perhaps the most similar figure is Ines Orsini, the protagonist of the film *Cielo sulla Palude* (*Heaven over the Marshes*), in the guise of a peasant girl. [40]

---

[39] Acts of the Apostolic Process, 308.
[40] Ciomei, *Il Pugnale*, 23-4.

10: A Portrait of Alessandro Serenelli

There are no long explanations regarding how the Goretti family recalled Alessandro, unlike how he recalled her. The most frequent adjectives were "shy, respectful, religious, lover of reading." Maria left us no portrait of her killer. The only words directed personally to Alessandro concern the salvation of his soul and the horror of such violence.

While there are no photographs of Alessandro in his youth, we have a detailed description of him. Specialists appointed by the Court of Rome for the October 1902 trial described Alessandro in great detail.

> The subject stands at 1.62 meters (5'4"); he is short, but not excessively. His constitution is robust, with a normal frame, pink skin, sufficiently nourished, and of pleasant physiognomy. Regarding his psychic functions, no characteristics of any disorder were detected. The sense of ideation is ready, alive, and sufficiently rich. His ideas, while taking into account his lack of education and very low social level, are quite clear and lucid. As regards his logical formation of thought and carrying out of an action in conformity with a given predefined end, no alterations of any kind were detected. His memory is very good, both for past events and recent ones. Indeed, some particularities that would be forgotten by others quite quickly, because they are insignificant and devoid of interest, are remembered by Mr. Serenelli in a detailed and precise way, not having omitted any circumstances of time

and place in which they manifested themselves. The subject's attention is alive and lasting and can be directed actively and for a long time towards any object, whether the conception of consciousness is carried out at a point in the internal world or the external world. Regarding his sphere of feelings, the subject is not very sensitive. Every affective feeling toward his father and family does not appear to be well-developed. In conversations we had with him, and when we touched upon filial love and described the isolation in which he found himself with his father, he never manifested any great feeling of pain. Gratitude, love of gusto, truth, and of goodness are flawed. Instead, the fulfilment of his selfish tendencies always emerges. [41]

Another interesting portrait of Alessandro comes from the owner of the dry goods store in Conca.

> I met him and knew him very well because he often came to shop in our store. As a young man, he was well-developed and also discreet, but I didn't like him as a person. He was a curmudgeon. He wore his hat pulled halfway over his eyes and always looked at you in a mean way. I was twenty years old and enjoyed talking to other young folks. But he must have had a heart and ears of stone. Instead of answering and engaging politely, he looked at you sideways. I can say that I barely ever heard the tone of his voice. [42]

Thus far, we have reconstructed a portrait of Alessandro as seen by those who were witnesses of the heinous crime. Yet there is a story written "between the lines" in addition to the one known to everyone. Here, we are referring to psychological and sociological theories positing that human behavior is the manifestation of a genetic-cultural memory of remote evolutionary development. This presents the human personality as a "continuum" in the search for his or her own fulfillment. In this dynamic perspective, the present cannot be portrayed as detached from reality, isolated from the person's background. It is often the synthesis, the updating, or even the overcoming of it. Thus, the consideration of an individual's past does not just mean analyzing an event that happened. Their genetic code and cultural environment are seen as determining variables regarding one's behavior.

Regarding Alessandro Serenelli, he was a complex and contradictory character. In fact, two apparently opposing attitudes emerge: fault and redemption. No one denies that he was responsible for a lurid and passionate crime. Yet he appears to have led a double life. He was violent in hatred but also overbearing in love. The twenty-year-old Serenelli, who on that afternoon of July 1902 becomes the protagonist of one of the most ferocious crimes of the era, apparently has nothing in common with the other Serenelli—the one who, on Christmas night 1934, begs Mamma Assunta for forgiveness.

Ines Orsini, the actress who played Maria Goretti in the film *Cielo sulla Palude* (*Heaven over the Marshes*), wrote about her experience meeting Alessandro. Her description captures well this dichotomy.

> I met Alessandro Serenelli in 1951 at the Capuchin convent of Ascoli Piceno. He was living there as a layman after having served twenty-seven out of thirty years for the murder of St. Maria Goretti. A few years earlier, I had finished shooting the film *Cielo sulla Palude* (*Heaven over the Marshes*). [...] The experience playing the lead role caused me to be hesitant regarding the person responsible for Maria's death. Before beginning the film, I had read the book on the life of Saint Maria Goretti and was particularly impressed. After having studied the script, a feeling of [self-] defense intensified in me, such that I even sought to avoid the young man (also a street artist) who played the role of Alessandro Serenelli. Strange feelings for a teenager! But let's return to the summer of 1951, when I was accompanied by a Franciscan friar to meet the real Alessandro Serenelli. I was surprised. He was not the feared young man I avoided during the shooting of the film but a mature, docile, humble man who had undergone the difficult journey of sincere repentance. He had atoned for the sin he committed in his youth. I remember his words. He told me [about the dream]. He said to me that I looked surprisingly similar to St. Maria Goretti. The memory of that encounter still remains alive in my mind. The man before me was humble, serene, and reconciled to

God and society. His face, that is, his persona bore nothing of the young man who had so violently taken the life of the saintly girl. Instead, Alessandro was a man who inspired tenderness and respect.

---

[41] Acts of the Civil Trial in Rome.
[42] Bruno Guerri, *Povera santa*, 105.

11: Dark Omens in the Cascina Antica

To better understand the viciousness of the attack, it is important to examine the relationship between Maria and Alessandro. Including the brief stint in Colle Gianturco, Marietta lived under the same roof as Alessandro for about three and a half years, a period of time not at all negligible. Breaking bread and living a communal life together would have contributed to the forging of more than an authentic friendship between Alessandro and Maria.

Alessandro had no brothers or sisters in Le Ferriere, and his "extended family" became like siblings. For example, Assunta said several times that she asked Alessandro to teach Marietta the rudiments of the alphabet. Throughout the year, the Goretti brothers participated with Serenelli in popular festivals such as the *merca*. Certainly, during the long winter evenings, among Giovanni's nodding off and Assunta's chores, sitting around the warm hearth created experiences of sharing and hope.

For these reasons, when on two separate occasions, he sought to violate her, these "strange requests" must have felt all the more devastating to Maria. Her points of reference would have collapsed. He had destroyed the trust and friendship that had developed among them.

The change began not long after the death of Luigi Goretti. When he died, the atmosphere in the Cascina Antica underwent a clear and inexorable decline. Assunta assumed her husband's place in the fields, while Marietta took on her mother's responsibilities of the housework and caring for the young children. From the perspective of work roles, the difficult situation seemed resolved.

However, the Goretti family's relationship with the Serenellis deteriorated.

Not accustomed to expressing their feelings and hardened by life's travails, the two Serenelli men never even conveyed their condolences to Assunta. On the contrary, Luigi's death triggered the disturbed psychology of the two men. After Luigi's burial, the elder Serenelli appropriated to himself the larger, more comfortable bedroom that Assunta had previously shared with her husband, forcing her to sleep in the bedroom with her daughters.

Despite the fact that he was not advanced in age, Giovanni looked terrible. He was ravaged by malaria and had one eyelid blocked by paresis, rendering his mien unsightly. His behavior was worse. On several occasions, after the death of Luigi, he made indecent proposals to Assunta. She indignantly rejected such advances that were absolutely contrary to her values. Her refusal angered Giovanni, who then became arrogant. He took the keys to the pantry, thus appropriating to himself the food and supplies. He also took the eggs from the henhouse, sold them, and kept the money for himself. It was as if he was asserting a tribal claim over the Goretti family and property.

Alessandro witnessed all this. His father's behavior likely triggered in him not only the process of identification but the idea that the balance of relationships were to be determined by force. It was a spiral that exacerbated the conflict in his relationships with people, especially of the opposite sex, and which can explain, in part, Alessandro's violent "deed."

Without justifying his actions his psychological profile can be understood better when considering the many negative conditions he endured: unstable relationships since childhood, frequent migrations, and constant precarious finances. Now, he was immersed in the merciless environment of the Pontine Marshes and subjected to his father's erratic behavior.

In contrast, there was the positive and brilliant example and nobility of the Gorettis. Though they suffered the same economic instabilities and depravity of the Pontine Marshes, they chose a different path. Paradoxically, Alessandro could have had a role model in Luigi, but the latter's premature death deprived him of the only authentic example to measure himself against.

Perhaps Alessandro was inspired by Luigi's positive attitude when he decided he wanted to become a cowhand. He had no aspiration to follow in his father's footsteps in the precariousness and monotony of field work. Becoming a cowhand—herding cattle and riding horses all day—was more legitimate in Alessandro's eyes. And with the salary of seven or eight lire per month, he would have earned considerably more than what a peasant made.

After gathering the courage, he went to the count's palace in Conca to express his desire. One could only imagine his tremendous disappointment when he heard the answer, "My joy will be complete when I finally rid myself of all Marchigian workers on my estates." [43]

---

[43] Bruno Guerri, *Povera santa*, 109.

12: Darkness Descends

The day Alessandro casually overturned a jug full of water in front of Marietta was the turning point. The climate in the Cascina Antica had been worsening by the day. Mario Cimarelli stated at the trial that "Serenelli was mistreating Maria Goretti in such a brusque manner that I never suspected he had any sympathy for her." [44] However, unbeknownst to family and neighbors, Alessandro attempted to violate her on at least two occasions before the attack.

Goretti scholars are not in agreement regarding when Alessandro's sordid attention towards Maria began. One source speaks of thirteen months prior to her martyrdom. Accordingly, after receiving her First Communion, she would have said to him, "Alessandro, think about what you are doing." Most likely, Alessandro's attempts date back to three to four months before he fatally stabbed her. Serenelli described the first attempt.

> The first time I tried to violate Maria was in the fields. Without saying anything, I approached her and embraced her. She freed herself from my arms, and we both got back to work. I told her not to say anything to anyone, though I didn't threaten her at that time. I had the impression that she understood my intentions, though she didn't say a word, and she maintained a prudent demeanor. Afterwards, she was reserved. I noticed that she tried to avoid me, though it was inevitable that we were near one another while working. [45]

The second attempt took place in the early afternoon among the silence of the Cascina Antica. While the adults were working outside and the children were sleeping, Marietta was tidying up Alessandro's room. He believed it was the perfect opportunity for him to achieve his aim. He threw Marietta down on the mattress and tried to rape her, but she managed to free herself. Fearing someone might enter, he left her alone. This time, however, he threatened her. "If you say anything to anyone, I will kill you." [46]

It was a brutal, explicit approach. Serenelli later admitted as much. He said:

> In attacking Maria's modesty, I had no other purpose than carnal release. I never had the thought of one day marrying her, especially since she was so young and I did not find her attractive. Nor did she ever lead me on with a smile or some other expression that would foster passion within me. She was so uninfluential over me that it was as if she was not in the house with me at all. Yet I never gave up the desire to achieve my goal. After the second attempt, the resolution to succeed in venting my passion was formed in my mind more than ever. At that point, I conceived the idea of killing her if she continued to oppose my desires. [47]

After the first of two "requests" (which, according to Alessandro, she didn't understand), the relationship between the two changed dramatically. The atmosphere was poisoned, and from that moment on she sought to avoid him. When Alessandro became aware of what was happening—that his desired goal was slipping away—he became frustrated and desired revenge. By then, Alessandro was hardened. He had entered a dark tunnel where reality and fantasy blurred.

Maria, on the other hand, remained quiet. She didn't say anything out of fear of his threats. She endured the most terrible ordeal of her life in complete solitude. She worried about what would become of her family if she revealed what was happening. Her mother was now financially dependent on the two Serenelli men. So she turned to prayer. Now consumed in a vortex bigger than herself, Marietta found refuge only in her faith. She said to her neighbor, Teresa Cimarelli, "Can we go to [church in] Campomorto tomorrow? I can't wait to receive Communion." [48]

Alessandro's resentment and Goretti's silence worked together to divert any suspicions Mamma Assunta may have had. Yet she noticed the changed dynamic between the two. She observed an angry reaction when he threw his shirt at Marietta, demanding that she mend it. She wisely said to her daughter, "Be patient. He'll be going away to the military soon [for obligatory service]."

But that was not enough. For Alessandro, his time of waiting had come to an end. It wasn't just an issue of impulsiveness but a total collapse of values that governed his conscience. Alessandro continued to pretend as if nothing was out of the ordinary, and he carried on normally. That is, until July 5, 1902—the day of infamy.

---

[44] Tarantini, *Maria Goretti*, 60.
[45] Ciomei, *Il Pugnale*, 27-8.
[46] Ibid., 28.
[47] Ibid.
[48] Alberti, *Maria Goretti*, 161.

13: The Passion of Maria Goretti

It was a particularly busy morning around the Cascina Antica, for this was the day for threshing fava beans. The sun was shining brightly in the sky, and there was a gentle breeze. Conditions were perfect for drying the beans at just the right point.

After lunch and a brief rest, work resumed. Before leaving the house, Alessandro told Maria, who was tidying up the kitchen, "There is a shirt of mine I need you to mend." When everyone was outside in the yard, Maria took a blanket and laid Teresa down on the upper landing of the stairs just outside the door leading to the kitchen. She then sat next to her sister and began to mend Alessandro's shirt.

Under the sweltering July heat, Alessandro and Angelo repeatedly passed over the beans in their mule-driven buggies, while Assunta and her sons stuffed the beans into bags. Not far away, the Cimarelli family was busy doing the same work in the yard in front of their farmhouse. Half an hour after resuming work, Giovanni Serenelli—sickened with malaria—told Assunta that he needed to rest. He found some shade at the bottom of the stairs, and he lay down.

A few minutes later, Alessandro got down from his buggy and asked Mamma Assunta to take his place. He mumbled that he needed to go into the house for something or another, acknowledged his father, and headed up the stairs. He passed Marietta on the landing arrogantly, went inside, and headed to the storeroom. Alessandro described the scene in detail:

> I took a sharp awl—one that Luigi Goretti had brought

from the Marches to make brooms—and I laid it on the external right corner of the cover of a chest just inside the kitchen to the right. [Editor: An awl is a long, pointed tool used to punch holes in wood or pick ice.] Then I went to the door and asked Marietta to come inside the house. She did not answer or move. So I then grabbed her roughly by the arm, but she resisted. I dragged her into the kitchen, which was the first room when you entered, and kicked the door shut, closing the latch, which was accessible only on the inside. She realized immediately that I wanted to repeat the same advance as on the two previous occasions and told me, "No, no! God does not want this! If you do this, you will go to Hell!" That's when I knew she was determined not to give in to my cruel cravings. I became enraged and grabbed the awl. I started striking her on her stomach, as you do when beating corn. I remember well that when I lifted Maria's clothes, she struggled to cover herself. She kept doing this while shouting, "What are you doing, Alessandro? You'll go to Hell!" I remember seeing blood, also on her clothes, and I left her while she was still struggling. But I knew I had struck her mortally. I threw the weapon inside the kitchen chest and went into my room. I shut myself in and climbed on the bed. [49]

After Alessandro slammed the door to his room, an eerie silence filled the air. Then, little Teresa awoke and began to cry loudly. With her remaining strength, Marietta dragged herself to the door and called out in a weak voice to the elder Serenelli, who was resting at the bottom of the stairs, "Come up here! Alessandro tried to kill me!"

Teresa's inconsolable wails could then be heard over the ruckus of the threshing. Concerned at Marietta's disappearance, Assunta asked her son, Mariano, to go and check on her. But Giovanni Serenelli had already arrived. When he saw Marietta lying bloodied on the floor, he shouted out to Assunta and then to Mario Cimarelli, who was working in the farmyard next door.

"My goodness! What is going on in my house?" Assunta muttered as she rushed down from the wagon. Mario arrived quickly. A panicky Giovanni Serenelli stammered, "She says my

Alessandro tried to kill her, but my Alessandro is not even here. It must have been Assunta's Alessandro."

The scene now was one of frenzied commotion. Cimarelli picked up the severely wounded girl, carried her to her bedroom, and laid her on the bed. He pleaded for his wife, Teresa, to run and get some vinegar as Maria was now unconscious.

Assunta later described what she witnessed:

> I followed Marietta, who was being carried into the bedroom. I immediately suspected that my little girl had been raped by Alessandro, who was not there. I lifted up her clothes to verify what I thought had happened. Instead, I saw that she had been butchered in the abdomen, and her insides were protruding. I screamed, and Cimarelli and the others took me out to the upper landing at the top of the stairs, where I fainted.

At this point, the scenario reached a fever pitch. Teresa Cimarelli returned with vinegar and managed to rouse Mamma Assunta.

"Teresa, they killed my daughter," the hysterical mother screamed. Soon afterwards, Marietta showed some signs of life, and the truth began to come to light.

"Marietta, what happened to you? Who did this to you?" they asked.

"It was Alessandro. He wanted to do bad things to me, which I did not want to." Then Assunta screamed.

When Alessandro's father encountered Assunta at the upper landing, he said to her in a state of shock, "It was not my Alessandro but yours who hurt her." [50] Alessandro Goretti was seven years old and sitting with his mother on the buggy at the time of the murder. Mario Cimarelli could not contain his anger, and he lashed out angrily at Serenelli. Afterwards, they took Assunta into the Cimarelli farmhouse.

"Teresa," moaned Marietta, "I want to be alone with you. Take me out of here. For Heaven's sake, do not let Alessandro come back!" Teresa Cimarelli changed Maria's bloodied clothes and bandaged her wounds, while Marietta kept repeating, "Alessandro, how sad you are; you're going to go to Hell!"

"What did Alessandro do to you, Marietta?" Teresa asked

gently.

"He wanted to do bad things to me, and I told him no! So he kept hitting me over and over." [51]

Meanwhile, Domenico Cimarelli raced to Conca to alert Count Mazzoleni and to borrow a horse to go call the doctor. Likewise, Mario Cimarelli went to Nettuno to get the family doctor, Dr. Bartoli, and to alert the Carabinieri (police). Before hurrying to the Cascina Antica, Count Mazzoleni informed the Carabinieri who were stationed in Cisterna and requested that the Red Cross of Carano come urgently.

While Maria was being tended to in her bedroom, an eerie silence prevailed in the other wing of the Cascina Antica. Alessandro had closed his bedroom door and refused to open it. He later stated:

> I threw the weapon behind the chest and went into my room. I closed the door and pulled the cord inside to [lock the door and] protect myself from the rage of the people. Then I lay down on my bed, waiting for the police to arrive. I thought it would be useless to try to escape. I heard voices different from those who had initially gone to Maria after hearing her cries. I recognized the voice of my father, of Maria's mother, and of some neighbors. [52]

News of the abominable crime spread quickly throughout the swampland of Le Ferriere. Dozens of people rushed to the Cascina Antica intent on carrying out "people's justice." The people of the marshes had a code of honor that did not permit people to trample over others with impunity.

One of Count Mazzoleni's watchmen, Nicola Antimo Romagnoli, played an important role throughout the aftermath of the crime. He heard the commotion and rushed to the Cascina Antica, where he discovered what had happened. He went to Alessandro's room and noted the door was locked. To prevent him from escaping, he blocked the door from the outside. Mazzoleni later sent more guards to stand over his door while they waited for the Carabinieri to arrive. Meanwhile, farmers armed with shotguns and pitchforks surrounded the farmhouse.

Shortly afterwards, the Carabinieri arrived from Carano. They arrested Alessandro and shielded him from the angry mob. Before he left, he told Count Mazzoleni where to retrieve the bloody awl. They led him out of the threshold of the door and descended the staircase. As he passed by the people, he saw their eyes full of hatred and desirous of revenge. Handcuffed and tied to two horses, he was led away on foot beyond the Astura River.

Dr. Ernesto Baliva of the Red Cross of Carano and Dr. Bartoli of Nettuno arrived almost simultaneously. They medicated little Maria as much as possible, and both agreed that she needed to go to the hospital in Nettuno urgently. Carried out on a stretcher, Marietta passed through the door at the upper landing. She was carried down the staircase in a semiconscious state, while her eyes were full of tears and anguish. She and Mamma Assunta were placed in the horse-drawn ambulance that made its way to Nettuno. As a grim reminder of what had just transpired, Alessandro's shirt lay there on the landing, never mended.

Marietta's face was ashen white. She was so innocent that she felt sorry for causing so much trouble for all these people. She always tried to do everything quietly. As the ambulance crossed the rickety bridge over the Astura River, local farmers uncovered their heads out of respect—a custom normally reserved for the feast of Corpus Christi.

No one slept or ate in the Cascina Antica that night. The Goretti siblings were graciously welcomed into the Cimarelli house. Yet their feelings of desperation were not over. The Cimarellis later said that they checked on the children throughout the night only to discover them wide awake and trembling with fear. Marietta was their entire world. Who knows what passed through the mind of Giovanni Serenelli as he passed the night by himself, completely alone, in the large Cascina Antica?

---

[49] Alberti, *Maria Goretti*, 164-5.
[50] Ibid., 180-1.
[51] Ibid., 167.
[52] Ibid., 170.

14: The Final Encounter

They had traveled together from Conca to Nettuno many times along that dirt road just beyond the Astura River. They went to the seaside city on Sundays and holy days or on market days and discussed many things as they walked. But on that July 5 afternoon, everything was different. She was the victim of an abominable crime, while he was the brutal executioner. She was riding inside a white horse-drawn ambulance, assisted by her mother, while he was handcuffed, chained between two horses. She was going to the hospital in Nettuno, while he was going to prison. Alessandro spoke of that awful moment.

> A good while after the "deed," two Carabinieri officers arrived together with Mazzoleni and Domenico Cimarelli. The Carabinieri asked me what I had done; they made me get down off the bed, and they put me in cuffs. They continued to ask me many questions, to which I kept saying, "I don't remember." Then we took the road to Nettuno: the Carabinieri went on horseback, and I was chained between them. [53]

As the ambulance slowly passed Alessandro and the officers on the road to Nettuno, Assunta looked at him through the window. "There's the killer," she thought to herself. Though lost in his thoughts, Alessandro could not have avoided seeing out of the corner of his eye that horse-drawn ambulance with the large red cross on its sides—the emblem of pain. That was the last contact he had with Marietta. He would not see her again; that is, not until she visited him in a dream in prison.

During the journey, the dialogue between Alessandro Serenelli and the Carabinieri officers became animated. Alessandro began to

plot his defense that he would assert during the trial. He stated:
> Along the way, the Carabinieri asked me how the event unfolded, and I told them everything, adding, however, that I didn't know what I was doing. To make them believe my story, I said that I had a brother in a mental hospital, and my mother had died of insanity. While this is true, I omitted the fact that her insanity occurred after my birth. I continued to play the insanity card during the subsequent interrogations and throughout the trial, though to no avail. It was easily discovered that I was not [insane]. [54]

The march from Le Ferriere to Nettuno lasted a couple of hours, but news of the heinous crime in Conca reached the city quickly. Curious onlookers flocked to see the murderer pass by. When Alessandro passed the threshing floor at Le Vignacce, there was open aggression. Despite the fact that his face was covered with a hat, he was recognized by Nocca Quinto, the owner of a restaurant, who knew him since he had brought eggs and chickens to sell there for two years. At a certain point, where the municipal building is now located, the anger was so palpable that there was the risk of a lynching. Branches and sticks, work tools, and stones were hurled at Alessandro, along with blasphemies and insults. Amidst the chaos, the officers initiated a gallop and quickly reached the barracks, which were about 200 meters away in what is now Piazza Mazzini.

Once arrived at the barracks, Alessandro was processed. Leonardo Ruggeri, the on-duty officer, documented the following:
> The arrested man had sweat dripping down his face, and I began to remove his shackles, though with difficulty due to damage to the padlock caused by dragging by the runaway horses. As soon as the shackles were removed, the prisoner asked for some water. I responded that anyone who had done such a thing did not deserve water. He replied that the "light had gone out of his eyes," and he did not know what he was doing. I had pity and gave him some water. [55]

The same officer later went to the Orsenigo Hospital to check on Maria's status. He said that he asked the little girl where she had been struck. "With her small hand, she indicated parts of her body. Then, modestly, she said, 'And also somewhere else,' without indicating the exact spot." ⁵⁶ The officer asked the doctors what message he should telegraph to his command in Rome; that is, whether the crime would be assault or murder. They replied that they would very likely not be able to save her.

Alessandro would never forget that first night as a prisoner—and not only because of the remorse that began to surface. A series of long and detailed interrogations began late at night. Brigadier Fantini asked, "Are you insane, or what, for doing such a thing?" Alessandro took the opportunity to reiterate that he "had an insane mother who died in a mental hospital in Ancona [and] a brother who is hospitalized in the same mental hospital." ⁵⁷

Around midnight, Leonardo Ruggeri wrote the following report, transcribed on July 7, 1902:

> My name is Ruggeri Leonardo di Filippo, aged twenty-three, from Florence, a Carabiniere officer of the Albano station, provisionally at the Nettuno station. On the current day, around 5:00 p.m., the commander of this station, Brigadier Fantini Lorenzo, informed by a certain Mario Cimarelli of the serious wounding of the girl Maria Goretti, which occurred on the Ferriere di Conca estate, at the hand of Alessandro Serenelli, ordered me and my fellow officer Adolfo Pierattini to go to the site and proceed to arrest Serenelli who was reportedly locked in his room. At full speed on our horses, we proceeded to the said estate. However, upon our arrival, Brigadier Beniamino Carpella and Officer Caprioli, having arrived a few minutes before us, together with the deputy of the Red Cross, were already putting the cuffs on Serenelli, and they had also seized the weapon. They handed Serenelli and the seized weapon over to us, and we transported him to Nettuno. Along the way, we asked Serenelli how the act had unfolded. He related to us that he had previously proposed to the Goretti girl that she should have relations with him but to no avail. Therefore, that morning to induce her to the same [act], he had attempted to have sexual intercourse with her, and at Goretti's rejections, he struck her with the confiscated awl, without knowing what he was doing. And to make us believe that he had

committed the crime in a moment of mental insanity, he stated that he had a demented brother locked up in a mental hospital and that his mother had died of mental illness. [58]

Meanwhile, an angry crowd revolted throughout the night, while the officers strained to hold them back. Elsewhere, "pilgrims"' headed towards the Orsenigo Hospital, where the status of little Maria was more and more pessimistic. The eyes of all stared at the small window, which remained illuminated all night. It was an extreme attempt to ward off that darkness that was darker than the moonless night.

---

[53] Ciomei, *Il Pugnale*, 35.
[54] Informative Process, 109.
[55] Tarantini, *Maria Goretti*, 65.
[56] Ibid.
[57] Ibid.
[58] Alberti, *Maria Goretti*, 170.

15: The Death of a Saint

The Divine Providence Hospital, also known as Orsenigo, was on the outskirts of Nettuno. It was founded by the religious community known as Fatebenefratelli, who administered it for twenty years. Maria arrived there at 8:00 p.m. on July 5. Before entering the operating room, the chaplain, Fr. Martino Guijarro, with the consent of Mamma Assunta, heard the girl's confession.

Throughout this period, it was as if Marietta entered into a new dimension. She continued to speak of the gravity of Alessandro's deed, and she was concerned about his eternal fate. She continued speaking of the true meaning of life, which is not one of human logic but of the difficult logic of forgiveness.

Given her condition, anesthesia could not be administered. Doctors Bartoli, Perotti, and Onesti performed an operation, which took place quickly and ended around 10:00 p.m. This is how Bartoli recalls it.

> I discovered that she had been struck in several parts of the abdomen and torso, just as the later autopsy confirmed, and her heart had been injured. During the treatment, I noticed that she prayed to Our Lady and retained her calm. I do not recall the precise words pronounced by Goretti, but her mental faculties were always very clear. [59]

Afterwards, Assunta was admitted into her room. Marietta immediately asked her mother, "How are my little brothers and sisters?" Then she calmed down and fell asleep. Assunta left the hospital around midnight, having been welcomed as a guest of the Donati family at Palazzo Enzoli, a short distance from the hospital. Throughout the night, her voice was increasingly fading, and there were nurses and police officers constantly coming and going.

THE DEATH OF A SAINT

In the morning, Assunta was permitted to return to the hospital and see her daughter again. In a weakened voice, she asked once again about her siblings and if she could see them again. At 10:00 a.m., the doctor came to check on Maria. He reported a significant decline. Meanwhile, Maria continued to pray, especially asking the intercession of the Virgin Mary.

Then the archpriest of the parish of San Giovanni in Nettuno, Msgr. Temistocle Signori, was called. He wished to administer the Eucharist. In an important moment, he asked Maria if she forgave her attacker.

"Marietta, do you forgive your killer?"

"Yes, I forgive him, and I want him close to me in Heaven." [60] This affirmation was vital. If there had not been forgiveness, there never would have been a Saint Maria Goretti. Instead, despite those horrendous circumstances, she revealed the maturity of her spiritual journey.

After she received Communion, she bowed her head and remained in prayer and intimate conversation with Jesus for a long period. She then received Extreme Unction.

By now, Maria had a high fever, and her face was white. When the doctors came in to check on her again, they prepared Assunta for the worst. But she already knew. She said she looked as pale as "St. Philomena." The doctors told her that Maria had severe internal hemorrhaging and she had developed septic peritonitis, that is, a serious bloodstream infection known more commonly as blood poisoning.

As Maria lay there in her final moments, in and out of consciousness, she experienced more delirium. In other moments, she was lucid, and she recalled her family, especially her baby sister, Teresa. She continued to ask why Alessandro had done such a thing, to reiterate that it was a sin, and that she wanted him to be with her in Heaven.

Suddenly, in a moment of clarity, gazing toward the door, she exclaimed, "What a beautiful lady!" As if she noticed the incredulity of those present, she added, "Is it possible you don't see her? Look! She is so beautiful, full of light and flowers!"

At 3:45 p.m., on July 6, 1902, Maria Goretti breathed for the last time. She was eleven years, eight months old. Her passion was over. Though it was a Sunday, she had just lived her Good Friday. Her resurrection would come soon enough.

After Maria's death, Mamma Assunta returned to Conca to be with her other children. None of them ever set foot in the Cascina Antica again. The Gorettis stayed as guests of the Cimarelli family, who helped Assunta put her affairs in order. She did not attend the funeral.

The funeral took place on the morning of July 8. The Mass was celebrated in the hospital chapel by Fr. Temistocle Signori. All the city's priests were present, including Fr. Basilio Morganti, who had administered Maria First Communion one year earlier. Also present were the Fraternity of the Most Holy Sacrament, pupils from the city's boarding schools, the Daughters of Mary Association (of which Marietta had become a member on her deathbed), and other groups. Many of the faithful waved palm branches, a symbol of martyrdom.

After the Mass, a slow procession meandered through the city to the sad sound of the bells. When the faithful reached the small church of Santa Croce in Via Santa Maria, the procession paused, and Fr. Temistocle gave another rousing sermon. He invited those present to pray for the intercession of Maria Goretti before God. She was then buried in the municipal cemetery, free of charge.

Assunta recalled that after initially receiving condolences, people soon began to pass to congratulate her as the special mother of a saint. The people were deeply moved by the story of the country girl who came from the marshes of hell to die along the shores of the city of Nettuno and how she forgave her killer. Those were unforgettable words of an extraordinary story. However, the human pen will not write the final word.

---

[59] Alberti, *Maria Goretti*, 174.
[60] Ibid., 176.

16: The Ferocity of Alessandro

On the day of Maria's funeral, a Roman newspaper, *Il Messaggero*, ran the following headline, "Human Beast Commits a Heinous Crime in Nettuno." The article covered the event and crime extensively. Against convention, extensive excerpts from the funeral and attack were published.

What Alessandro did on July 5, 1902 was brutal. The ferocity of the attack left the doctors at the Orsenigo hospital astonished. The autopsy was performed by Doctors Impallomeni and Bartoli. Follows is a transcription of the report. We left the clinical language the way it was written. Though it is cold, it captures well the viciousness of the attack.

The Autopsy:

> By means of a straight median cut conducted from the chin to the pubis, leaving the navel on the right, we divide the skin and subcutaneous tissue.
>
> The abdominal cavity:
>
> From below the navel we understand in the cut the one already done for the laparatomy: we cut into it followed the entire abdominal wall until the corresponding cavity was exposed. Meanwhile, we make sure of the normal position that all the viscera occupy and we see a notable quantity of cloudy, bloody liquid, which partly pours out of the cut just made.
>
> From a careful examination of the abdominal viscera and the internal wall, the following appears: parietal and visceral peritoneum (of the intestinal loops) hyperemic, vascularized.
>
> Fibrino-purulent exudate on the intestinal loops:

1-2) Two puncture wounds to the intestine: that is, one on the anterior surface of the last portion, and the other on the ileum: both not sutured and extended approximately five millimeters each.

3) One wound from the tip of the parietal peritoneum in the left lumbar region (see wound number 10).

4-5-6-7) Four puncture wounds in the parietal peritonen in the lower pelvis—limited to the superior strait—two on each side.

8-9) Two puncture wounds corresponding to the parietal attachment of the mesentery.

The injuries referred to in Nos. 1-2-4-5-6-7-8-9 correspond to the four wounds reported on the abdomen and precisely where the laparotomy occurred.

Considerable quantity of pure blood, mostly coagulated in the lower pelvis.

Emptied stomach. Liver of normal volume, slate (?) color, and nutmeg-colored cuts (degenerations).

Spleen enlarged more than double, pulpable.

Normal-healthy kidneys.

A small intestinal worm (lombricus), still alive, was noticed as soon as the abdomen was opened, and it emerged from one of the two wounds of the same loops.

Peritoneum and tissues adjacent to the chirurgical incision [are] red and congested. Normal uterus and ovaries.

Thoracic cavity. [We] loosened the skin and muscles of the front wall of the chest to form two large lateral flaps, and we uncover the bone wall—ribs and sternum—and notice that meanwhile, on the second right rib, there is a small lesion from a pointed weapon (a strike) but not piercing the rib itself (see wound no. 3).

Having removed the sternum with the costal cartilages, after disarticulation of the clavicles (sterno-clavicular joint), we uncover the thoracic cavity. The following is the result of our observations:

Liquid and coagulated blood in small quantities in the left pleural cavity.

No. 6 puncture wounds on the left lung = of which three

on the back and three on the left lateral surface; essentially, however, they are three transfixed wounds of the same lung (from back to front). No. 3 wounds on the left posterior chest wall (corresponding to the three noted on the posterior surface of the lung), of which the first corresponds to the seventh rib, perforated and chipped: the second corresponds to the tenth rib also chipped; and the third in the eleventh intercostal space = this last corresponds to a lesion of the dome of the diaphragm (wound perforating the diaphragm and communicating with the abdominal cavity) (see external wounds described in numbers 4-5- 6-7-8-9 and the letters a.c.d.e. = the two next wounds d,e penetrate the thorax through a single opening).

Contused puncture wound of the pericardium posteriorly and corresponding posterior wound of the right auricle.

Little blood in the pericardial cavity.

Empty heart cavity.

Large vases, even empty ones.

Healthy heart in all its parts.

Right lung intact and healthy.

Thymus gland of normal volume.

Cranial and oral cavity: Once the cranial vault is sawed off and removed, the meninges and first the dura mater are revealed, which offers nothing remarkable with the semi-empty sinuses. Arachnoid and pia meninges are also normal with mild hyperemia.

Brain in advanced cadaveric decomposition. Cutting reveals nothing abnormal.

Having examined the mouth, the pharynx, and the larynx, we do not find anything that could recall facts of violent action exerted on these parts.

After this [examination], we uniformly and unanimously judge and conclude:

First: Goretti Maria suffered fourteen wounds from a perforating weapon and others incidentally and four light bruises. Of these external wounds, four penetrated the chest and damaged the pericardium, the heart (right auricle), and the left lung, as well as the diaphragm; five penetrated the abdominal cavity and damaged the small intestine and the ileum, as well as the mesentery.

Second: The weapon used was a long and narrow one, pointed and partially bent.

Third: The sole and absolute cause of the death of the young girl just autopsied (Goretti Maria) was septic peritonitis due to intestinal wounds, as well as severe hemorrhage produced by the numerous wounds.

Fourth: Death, due to the characteristics shown by the corpse, dates from twenty-four hours. Impallomeni Dr Giuseppe Bartoli Dr Francesco

Nettuno, July 7, 1902. [61]

---

[61] Tarantini, *Maria Goretti*, 69-70.

17: Regina Coeli

In that era, the Carabinieri barracks of Nettuno were located outside the medieval village—in today's Piazza Mazzini—on the road to Anzio. Interrogations continued until the first light of dawn, when orders came in to take the prisoner to a prison in Rome. Formalities in Rome were wrapped up in the early morning, and Alessandro was accompanied on the 11:10 a.m. train.

Once again, Carabinieri officers shielded the prisoner from the angry crowd, and the arrival at the train station was a relief for shackled Alessandro. The Nettuno railway station was just about 200 meters from the hospital. Maria likely did not hear the whistle blow when the train left the station, but Alessandro knew everything. It is believed that as the train rattled by the hospital, Marietta was forgiving her killer.

After an hour's journey by train from Nettuno, the military escort reached Rome's Termini station. The military convoy left the station and traveled along Via Nazionale past Piazza Venezia, along the Corso Vittorio, over the Tiber River on the Ponte der Sordino bridge (now demolished), and along Via della Lungara. Of course, Alessandro never saw anything. There were no windows in the *cellulare*, or prison transport vehicle. Finally, they reached the Trastevere district.

Alessandro was processed in the storied prison known as Regina Coeli. The prison once served as a monastery for nuns. According to an old tradition, its name derives from the fact that in 1654, the nuns would pause to recite the Regina Coeli (Queen of Heavens) prayer every four hours. After [the Capture of Rome and the Unification of Italy in] 1870, the Regina Coeli became the primary prison in Rome. Regina Coeli was no longer an oasis of peace. It was hellish.

Everything was about to change for Alessandro. The bucolic rhythms of agricultural life in the countryside were about to give way to the hardships of rigid prison life. Moreover, a gnawing sense of remorse was beginning to swell up within him. Alessandro spoke about his arrival in Rome.

> I was transferred from Nettuno to Rome, then to Regina Coeli, on July 6. I was placed in solitary confinement, where I spent hours of awful discomfort. I spent days weeping because I was now aware of everything that had happened. And I knew it was all my fault. I had some bitter reflections, but it was now too late. On July 8, I was interrogated by the investigating judge and afterwards many other times by judges and lawyers. It had become a torment for me. [62]

Alessandro spent the first few months in Regina Coeli in solitary confinement. The interminable silence was only broken by conversations with judges and his lawyers. Otherwise, there was only the pealing of the myriad bell towers of the Eternal City.

At the end of July, Alessandro had a visitor. He recalled, "Before the trial, I had only one visitor: my father. He was devastated, the poor man! He brought me a basket of fruit. He encouraged me and gave me some money. After he left, I never saw him again." [63] This nostalgic reminiscence is a reminder that the perpetrator of the heinous crime was someone's son. He was still loved by his father.

---

[62] Ciomei, *Il Pugnale*, 36.
[63] Ibid., 37.

18: The Motive

At the beginning of the twentieth century, criminal trials in Italy were regulated by the Code of 1865, which came into force on January 1, 1866. Similar to European legislation of the era, the Italian criminal procedure consisted of two phases: a preparatory phase referred to as "Instruction," in which evidence was collected and would serve as the basis of the actual judicial procedure, and a second Judicial Phase, which was the trial itself and which culminated in conviction or acquittal.

The Instruction phase was usually preceded by a preliminary Instruction, entrusted to the judicial police or conducted by the public prosecutor himself. This phase was extremely basic when the accused admitted guilt. During this phase, the defendant's lawyer could not intervene. Only at a later time was he able to view the documents and contact his client. Therefore, this phase always had a secret, written character, and the statements made had considerable importance as they were not contaminated by outsiders.

The criminal trial consisted according to the norms en force then of a first-degree trial and an appellate trial, which could be followed by a third trial, consisting however of a judgment of mere legitimacy. The trial phase was public and oral, and the role of the defense attorney was more prominent, as he was now tasked with demonstrating to the judges the circumstances of the facts and the legal issues pertaining to the trial.

When the accused had confessed (as was the case with Alessandro), the trial was not so much to ascertain the truthfulness of the facts as to clarify the legal perspective of the facts. An emphasis was placed on the state of mind of the accused, including, when appropriate, expert opinions on the accused's free will and capacity of understanding—especially as insanity could lead to acquittal. Given the strong emotions and interest of the people, due to the age of the victim, and given the media sensation, both the preliminary investigation phase and the criminal trial were conducted with great rigor.

In the aftermath of Marietta's death, the Judicial Authority, represented by Sir Francesco Basso and the chancellor Lucchesi, went to Le Ferriere for the legal investigations and invited Mamma Assunta to file charges. On that occasion, the expertise evaluation on the Cascina Antica was compiled. The same investigating judge, Francesco Basso, began interrogating the murderer on the afternoon of July 8.

Two well-known celebrity defense attorneys from Rome were appointed to represent Alessandro: Cano-Lintas and Dante Veroni. During the preliminary investigation phase, Alessandro stated a mix of truth and lies due to his need to defend himself and the confusion that was swirling within. Immediately after the crime, he came up with a defense strategy. He drew on his family history of mental illness by mentioning his mother and brother. Now, after just eleven days, before the Council Chamber at the Civil and Criminal Court of Rome, Serenelli declared "his guilt for both crimes ascribed to him by accepting that he had killed Goretti [falsely] to live without working at the expense of the Treasury [of the Kingdom of Italy]." [64]

Follows is the report from the interrogation of Alessandro Serenelli rendered on July 8, 1902, in Regina Coeli. The graphic language has not been edited.

> My name is Alessandro Serenelli, son of Giovanni and the late Cecilia Mengoni, aged 20 from Paterno (Ancona) and resident in the Roman countryside, Ferriere di Conca, literate farmer, unmarried, never convicted of a crime, never served in the military. *When questioned about the accusation made against him*: I had been working with my father for four years on the estate of Sir Attilio Mazzoleni, and I lived in the farmhouse together with the widow Assunta Casagrande [sic], mother of six children, who cultivated the same land. One day last June, taking

advantage of her absence, I tried to have carnal contact with her first daughter, Maria Goretti. I went so far as to lift her skirt, taking my virile rod out of my trousers, but the Goretti girl resisted, and while allowing her to leave the rural house where we were, I ordered her not to tell her mother anything, telling her that otherwise I would kill her. This was a momentary whim, and no such thought ever again arose in my mind. Seeing that despite my work, I was always in poverty, a few days before the fifth [day] of this month, I made the decision to kill the Goretti girl to go to prison and live at the expense of the [state] Treasury. In fact, on the fifth of this month, around 3:00 p.m., while I was threshing beans in the farmyard with a cart pulled by two oxen, I got off the cart and had [Assunta] Casagrande, who was following me and shucking the beans, get on it, and I told her to continue the work for me because he needed to go into the house. As I passed my father, who was sitting near the stable, I asked him how he felt, since I knew he was unwell. He replied that he still had a fever. I entered the house without saying anything to the Goretti girl, who was seated on the landing, mending one of my shirts. I went to the last room on the right, which was used as the warehouse where, among other things, there were some old tools, and I took a sharp awl that Luigi Goretti had brought from the Marches to [make] brooms, and I placed it in the external corner to the right of the cover of an extant chest in the kitchen, on the right as you enter. Then I dragged Maria Goretti by the arm into the kitchen and closed the door just with the horizontal latch that is on the inside. I lifted Goretti's skirt from the front not because I wanted to attack her honor but to better lead to effect my design, that is, to ensure that the tip of the weapon was in immediate contact with Goretti's body without the impediment of her clothes. Goretti, supposing that I wanted to attack her honor again, was frightened and showed that she wanted to give in to my lascivious desires, but since my thought was to sacrifice her for the aforementioned purpose, without her ever having to commit any fault towards me, I took hold of the awl, and knocking her to the ground, I struck her with blows on her bare abdomen. The Goretti girl managed to get up and call her mother for help, and while she turned her back to me, I struck her with even more blows on the spot. Since she had fallen to the ground, I believed her to be dead, and therefore, having retreated to my room, I closed the door by pulling in the cord to escape the wrath of the people, and I lay down on my bed waiting for the Carabinieri to come and arrest me. While lying in bed, I heard a knock on the door several times, but I didn't open it. With a shove, my father opened the door and asked me what I had done, but I didn't answer him. When the Carabinieri arrived, they immediately put iron cuffs on my wrists. They asked me where I had placed the wounding weapon, and I also did not answer. Then Mr. Mazzoleni ordered me to speak, and I pointed to the aforementioned chest behind which I had thrown the awl immediately after the crime. I confirm that I killed Maria Goretti without any reason, based on a plan formulated by me before the act, but I declare that I now regret the act committed. I confirm once again that I once attempted to have intercourse with Goretti. [65]

In this initial formal statement, Alessandro blatantly lied. He stated that he killed Maria not because she had resisted his attempts to violate her but because he wanted to be cared for by the government. This admission is confirmed by the requisition of the King's Attorney General to the prosecution section for referral before the Assize Court of July 22, 1902. However, the judge did not believe his alibi.

> Considering, given the above, with the facts set out, as well as the findings of the general case, [the following] are specifically demonstrated by the precise confessions made, which concord with the findings the victim made immediately after the fact and constantly repeated until her death, as well as with what the witnesses examined have testified; Considering that the homicidal intention is evident, having regard to the quality of the weapon used, the number and ferocity of the blows directed at most vital

organs; Nor can there be any doubt that the accused acted with premeditation, as he himself acknowledged in his interrogation and as, moreover, can be deduced from all the details of the above-mentioned fact, and in particular from the circumstance that, before attempting to rape Goretti, Serenelli availed himself of the awl, which he placed on the chest within easy reach; Which clearly reveals the plan he had already devised to sacrifice the young girl if she did not surrender to his lascivious desires; Considering that, instead of the qualification of the accused of aggravating circumstances, the other one would seem better corresponding to the findings acquired during the Instruction, provided for by no. 6 of article 366 c.p. of the Criminal Code, namely that the murder of Goretti was committed immediately after the crime of attempted sexual intercourse, due to the failure to achieve the intent. In fact, although it is true that the accused said during the judicial interrogation that he had no intention of giving vent to his lusts but that he killed the Goretti girl because, being poor, he wanted to live at the expense of the Treasury, it is no less true, on the other hand, that the opposite is evident not only from the repeated declarations of the victim but from what the accused himself espoused, immediately after the act, to Carabiniere Leonardo Ruggeri. The version therefore that Serenelli, motivated by an impetus of lust, sacrificed Goretti since he had not achieved his proposed intent, is the most acceptable, also because it is the most likely, while the meditated responses given later to the Instruction judge are colored by a character of exceptional strangeness, which was perhaps related to defenses. [66]

A third motive was suggested by the defense—the classic one that often takes place in trials of sexual violence: provocation on the part of the woman and her consent. But on this point Serenelli never yielded, "Never did Maria give me the slightest opportunity to reawaken my passion, not with a smile, nor with any ambiguous expression." [67]

On August 14, 1902, the Section of the Court of Appeal of Rome, not believing the defense, which tried to mitigate his guilt,

issued the following accusation:
> Proceedings against Alessandro Serenelli, arrested, accused of first-degree attempted rape and second-degree premeditated murder with aggravating circumstances. Given that the following facts remain established in the documents of the case: [namely, that Alessandro Serenelli murdered Maria Goretti]. In specific terms, the accused is burdened first of all by his own confession, indeed by explicitly declaring himself the actor of the two crimes. Given that the first fact reveals the characteristics of the crime envisaged by article 61.331.333 penal code, since for the findings outlined above, Serenelli is exuberantly suspected of having attempted with suitable means to force the unfortunate girl, who was just eleven years old, into carnal union, abusing the domestic relationships that interceded with one another, because they were cohabiting in the same house as if one family. If he was unable to achieve his aim, this happened due to circumstances beyond his control and precisely due to the resistance put up by the girl. Given that the elements of the crime envisaged by Articles 364.366, nos. 9 and 6 of the said code. Indeed, the homicidal intention is evident from Serenelli's own confession and is in perfect consonance with the violence and repetition of the blows, with the parts [of the body] targeted, with the quality of the instrument used. As for premeditation, it can also be deduced from the accused's confession, in perfect harmony with all the circumstances under which the grim event took place, which clearly demonstrate that he had coldly deliberated and premeditated the atrocity in the event, which actually occurred, that the intended victim resisted. And because he ultimately committed the atrocity because he was unable to achieve his intended goal. And that this was the determining cause of the crime is clear from the first statements given by Serenelli to Carabiniere Ruggeri immediately after committing it, since it was not possible to have regard to the retraction he made later, because such retraction was not justified, and because, on the other

hand, the new version given by him is not supported in the slightest by the results of the trial, which, on the contrary, support and make the first version more plausible than ever. The aggravating circumstance of brutal malvagity therefore falls by itself, hence the epigraph, which must be more correctly replaced by the one just mentioned. Given that these are crimes within the jurisdiction of the Court of Assizes, in application of article 9.437 of the code of penal process (the Court) accuses Alessandro Serenelli, son of Giovanni: first, of having in June 1902, on the Ferriere di Conca estate ... (with abuse of domestic relations), with the aim of forcing the eleven-year-old girl Goretti Maria into sexual intercourse, begun, with suitable means, the execution of this act, but not having done everything that was necessary to consumption due to circumstances beyond his control; and second, of having on the fifth day of July 1902 in the aforementioned locality, with the aim of killing, with premeditation, and for not having been able to achieve the intended purpose of carnal conjunction with the said girl Maria Goretti, caused the latter's death by repeatedly inflicting blows on her with a sharp pointed instrument, and producing injuries that were the unique and absolute cause of her death which occurred the following day. [The Court] orders the referral of the accused before the Court of Assizes of Rome and issues an arrest warrant for him. [68]

At this point, the only practicable defense for the accused was to request a psychiatric evaluation. On September 30, 1902, Serenelli's two defense attorneys sent a formal request for a psychiatric report, as shown in the documents of the criminal trial.

Serenelli's lawyers asked that the appraisal be carried out by Professor Giovanni Mingazzini (1859–1929), a prominent Italian neurologist of such prestige that he is referenced in the Italian Encyclopedia. For its part, the Court officially summoned to the same hearing Prof. Nicola de Pedys, who also participated in the aforementioned session. This occurred on the basis of Article 152 CCP. The report was drawn up and then presented at the hearing on October 15 and bears the signature of the two doctors.

[64] Tarantini, *Maria Goretti*, 95.
[65] Ibid., 82-3.
[66] Ibid., 95-8.
[67] Informative Process, 172.
[68] Ibid., 98-100.

19: The Trial

From Regina Coeli prison, Alessandro was accompanied in the Carabiniere prison transport vehicle along Via della Lungara 169, over Ponte Mazzini, along Largo Perosi, then Via dei Cartari, to Piazza della Chiesa Nuova. Once again, he never saw any of it. On the other hand, bystanders stopped to gawk as the windowless military vehicle passed by. His trial was the most sensational since the monetary scam involving the failed Banca Romana that had taken place a few years earlier, in 1893.

The trial began at 9:00 a.m. on Saturday, October 11, 1902, in the Public Hearing hall of the Court of Rome. In that era, jurors were not selected randomly among the common citizens (who were mostly illiterate), but were drawn by lot from a selected list provided by the Court, which was renewed every fortnight. The list regarding Alessandro Serenelli had been extracted for the period October 7–22, 1902, and included forty ordinary jurors and ten alternates, including twenty employees of state ministries, five engineers, three lawyers, a doctor, a pharmacist, two city councilors, two law graduates, two professors (physics and literature), two solicitors, school teachers, and specialists. Within the fortnightly list, there was a rotation from trial to trial: there were twelve who judged Alessandro Serenelli. The questions posed to them by the Court to establish Alessandro's guilt were nine. Decisions were made based on majority.

In the first session, in addition to the composition of the jury and the completion of formalities, various witnesses were questioned. The next hearing was set for Monday, October 13. The session began, but since the psychiatric report was not ready, the trial was postponed for two days. In fact, the entire hearing was fully completed on Wednesday, October 15.

The first order of business in the morning of the fifteenth was the reading of the psychiatric report that Prof. Mingazzini had prepared after his evaluation of Alessandro. Follows is the report nearly in its entirety. In this report, Alessandro asserts a second lie that he would have to correct later.

> I pointed out to him that the idea that arose in his mind of killing someone in order to ensure bread for many years was an idea that must have come to mind after the crime, in order to mitigate his responsibility, while the reality of the fact is that he killed the girl because she did not want to give in to his carnal desires. To this, he replied:
>> I repeat, I was fixated on what was lacking [in my basic needs] and that I was seeking to ensure my bread. Therefore, seeing that there was no way for me to make a living for myself, the idea arose in me, especially after reading [the newspaper] *Il Messaggero*, which reports on crimes, that I could commit one myself so that I would not have to strive to make a living. I thought about these things every day, until that day, when seeing Maria mending my shirt, the thought arose in me of taking her life in order to thus achieve my goal of no longer having to struggle to get by. It is true that about a year ago, I propositioned Maria to engage in carnal acts to which she did not want to consent. However, it is certain that if she had reciprocated, I would not have had in my soul that anger that I had when I saw her, and therefore I would not have committed an offense against her. [During the first attempt,] at that time, the girl, frightened by my violence, immediately said, "Yes, yes." I assumed what she wanted to say to me was, "Don't hurt me; I consent." [After the crime,] I was then overcome by fear not only of the brother of the deceased, who is only thirteen or fourteen years old, but that the villagers and friends of the family might come and kill me.

> [The accused reveals] normal general sensitivities, normal reflexes, and normal functions of physiological organic life and functions of relational and reproductive life. He killed the Goretti girl solely because she did not want to comply with his carnal desires, and the proof of this is his own declaration, "it is certain that if she had reciprocated, I would not have had in my soul that anger that I had when I saw her, and therefore I would not have committed an offense against her." These words luminously demonstrate the true cause of the murder. [His aggression is born of] a morally degenerate and dissatisfied individual. He is the descendant of an insane mother and an alcoholic father, and subjects such as these possess [reduced] powers of criticism, inhibition, and self-control. Therefore, these hereditary conditions constitute an extenuating circumstance of culpability. [69]

Alessandro's defense lawyers summoned several witnesses to testify on his behalf: the Casoni brothers, Alessandro Pace, and Giuseppe Cherubini—all farmers from Conca. Brothers Fortunato and Rinaldo Casoni declared:

> Serenelli was of a very mild nature. He had epileptic attacks, dizziness, and vertigo a few days before the crime because he remained working on the threshing floor during the hottest hours of the day. His mind was therefore deranged or at least weakened when the crime was committed. [70]

Alessandro Pace, for his part, testified that "Serenelli was periodically attacked three or four times a year by very strong pains in his head, and during these exuberations he lost consciousness and committed the strangest acts of madness." [71] Giuseppe Cherubini limited himself to confirming what the others had declared.

Next, the prosecution's witnesses testified. Deserving special attention were Mario Cimarelli and his wife, his brothers Domenico and Antonio, Regina Medei, prison guards Angelo Cianchelli and Elio Mattei, and Carabiniere Ruggeri Leonardo. Assunta Goretti was present but not questioned as she was the injured party. Absent was Giovanni Serenelli.

Another important part of the trial was the awl. As the murder weapon, it attracted special interest from magistrates and investigators. There are several testimonies and statements. An interesting statement was given by an expert named Dr. Impallomeni. During the trial, he stated the following:

> The weapon is a type of awl with a wooden handle whitened with age. It is quadrilateral and rectangular in shape and gradually ends in a very sharp tip. About 5 centimeters (2 in.) from the tip, it is curved, but the tip is not blunt. The said awl is made of iron. It measures about 23.5 centimeters (9.2 in.) in length excluding the handle, 8 millimeters (.3 in.) in maximum width, and 5.5 millimeters (.21 in.) in maximum thickness. The corners of the tool are quite sharp but rounded at the tip. This shows that it was recently put to the millstone, as does the fact that rust largely covers it elsewhere. Among rust stains, blood stains can be discerned. The wounds found and described on the cadaver of Maria Goretti were evidently produced by the tool just described (or by another similar one) because their quality and shape are suitable to this type of weapon. The curvature discovered in it could have occurred both during the repeated blows inflicted on the victim and when the culprit threw the weapon on the ground. [72]

Beyond the technical language, the murder weapon also reveals the brutality of the martyrdom of St. Maria Goretti. The crooked tip captures the blind violence of the moment Alessandro stabbed Maria. His statement confirms the ferocity: "I began to strike her belly as when beating corn or chopping wood." [73]

---

[69] Tarantini, *Maria Goretti*, 106-7.
[70] Ibid., 103-4.
[71] Ibid., 104.
[72] Tarantini, *Maria Goretti*, 77-8.
[73] Alberti, *Maria Goretti*, 165.

20: Sentencing

Serenelli's final entry into the courtroom was marked by a hushed buzz. His hands and feet were shackled, his eyes were half closed, and he appeared dazed. He did not look at the public. Despite the fact that he knew Assunta was present, he reiterated his defense strategy—that he murdered Maria in order to be provided for at the expense of the state, and that she had given prior consent so as not to be killed.

After the psychiatric report was introduced, the possibility of inherited insanity was excluded. The jury then met in the Council Chamber. After just over two hours, the verdict as expressed by the majority was ready. Follows is the complete text of both the conviction and the sentence (taken from the minutes of the constitution of the jury and the hearing).

The sentence (October 15, 1902)
In the name of His Majesty Vittorio Emanuele III, by grace of God and by will of the King of Italy, the Court of Assizes of Rome pronounces the following
SENTENCE
in the case of the Public Prosecutor
Against
ALESSANDRO SERENELLI, son of Giovanni, aged 20, born in Paterno di Ancona, resident in "Le Ferriere di Conca" estate, farmer;
Arrested-
Accused:
First, of having, in June 1902, on "Le Ferriere di Conca" estate (Rome), with abuse of domestic relations, with the aim of forcing the eleven-year-old girl Goretti Maria into

sexual intercourse, begun, with suitable means, the execution of this act, having not completed everything necessary for its completion due to circumstances beyond its control (Articles 61, 331, 332 of the penal Proc. Cod.).

Second: of having, on the fifth day of July 1902, in the aforementioned location, with the aim of killing, with premeditation and for not having been able to achieve the intended purpose of carnally conjoining with the aforementioned girl Maria Goretti, caused the latter's death by repeatedly inflicting blows on her with an awl and producing injuries which were the sole and absolute cause of her death, which occurred the following day (Articles 364, 366 nos. 2 and 6 of the Penal Code.).

Since the jurors, with their verdict, found Alessandro Serenelli guilty of voluntary premeditated homicide, committed to facilitate the commission of another crime, that is, attempted rape with abuse of domestic relationships, to the detriment of Maria Goretti, eleven years old, with mitigating circumstances for the latter crime.

Since the first crime is punishable by life imprisonment, but since Serenelli is older than eighteen and younger than twenty-one, this penalty is replaced by imprisonment of twenty-five to thirty years, since the Court, considering the entire fact, believes it is right to set the maximum sentence, though it cannot be increased further for the other crime, the sentence of which remains absorbed.

Alessandro Serenelli is hereby sentenced to imprisonment for thirty years, after which completion, [he shall be] under the special supervision of the P.S. for three years, perpetually banned from [holding] public office, legally banned during the sentence, [obligated] to compensate the injured party for damages and to repay the expenses to the State Treasury.

Comm. Dionisio Vitelli (President)
Cav. Torello Serviei (Judge)
Nicola Giannattasio (Judge)
sign together with the Vice Chancellor of the hearing. [74]

The Conviction

The Ordinary Court of Assizes of Rome, composed of the sir magistrates:
Comm. Nicola Giannattasio (President)
Guido Mazzucchetta (Judge)
Giuseppe Zappia (Judge)
gathered in the Council Chamber
Having seen the sentence pronounced by this Court of Assizes on October 15, 1902
AGAINST
Alessandro Serenelli, son of Giovanni, born on June 2, 1882 in Paterno, with which he was sentenced to thirty years of imprisonment, plus accessories, for premeditated murder and attempted rape (Articles 364-366 and 331 of the Penal Code) committed in Rome in June and July 1902;
Having seen the request of the Attorney General dated October 28, 1925 [requesting that] the sentence imposed be applied to the indult granted by R. Decree July 31, 1925 no. 1277;
Since Serenelli has the right to benefit from the two-year conditional amnesty of the sentence of thirty years of prison, imposed on him with the aforementioned sentence, for the crime of murder, a penalty in which the sentence for the crime of attempted rape was declared absorbed, because the requirements required by Articles 4-5 and 9 of R.D. July 31, 1925 no. 1277 benefit his favor.
For these reasons, having seen article 590 of the Criminal Procedure Code;
Declares two years of the prison sentence conditionally pardoned in favor of Alessandro Serenelli imposed on him by this Court in the sentence of October 15, 1902. [75]

That interminable day ended with an unforgettable moment in

which Assunta Goretti was the protagonist. When asked by the President of the Court whether she forgave Alessandro, she replied without hesitation, "Yes, Mr. President, I forgive him." [76] Murmurs of amazement and indignation could be heard throughout the courtroom. Someone shouted out his disapproval [that she should not have forgiven Alessandro].

Assunta Carlini's reply was swift, "And if Jesus Christ were to do the same with us?" [77] In that hall, once destined for Palestrina's famous musical auditions, never had a voice risen so sublime and unattainable to the point of touching the strings of the Heart of the Almighty. The school of forgiveness begun by Marietta began to bear fruit, which culminated in the great forgiveness on Christmas night 1934.

Alessandro later recalled that dramatic day of October 15.

> Unfortunately, this was the sentence. [...]. I expected it as I received it, since those who accompanied me had told me this while we were going to court, but it was still a terrible blow. The interrogators were something terrible: they were exhausting, but I was never mistreated. The impression of the sentence, which I had foreseen, was horrendous: I would have preferred to be dead and buried. [78]

On the same day, Alessandro Serenelli filed an appeal to the Court of Cassation against the sentence. But three days later, October 18, he renounced his appeal and accepted the sentence. According to a census carried out shortly after the Breach of Porta Pia events, Italy had 27 million inhabitants, with a prison population of 55,800 people. For the next twenty-seven years, Alessandro Serenelli would be one of them.

---

[74] Tarantini, *Maria Goretti*, 107-8.
[75] Ibid., 109-10.
[76] Informative Process, 252.
[77] Ibid., 252.
[78] Ciomei, *Il Pugnale*, 36-7.

21: Press Coverage

The responses from the press were immediate and copious. Despite the fact that murder was more common in that era than today—between 1800 and 1881, the homicide rate was fifteen times higher than today—the crime that took place in the Cascina Antica struck the conscience of the people both for its ferocity and the young ages of the victim and the killer. Moreover, Conca's proximity to Rome, as well as Alessandro's trial that took place in the capital, led to greater coverage. Following are several articles that were published in the days after the event.

Il Messaggero, July 7, 1902
Second page, sixth column, top
Headline: *The Human Beast: The Brutal Crime in the Nettuno Countryside*

Those who have read *La Bête Humaine* (The Human Beast), written by Émile Zola in 1890, close the volume, nauseated by the brutal scenes described, and exclaim, "This cannot be possible." Yet the grim and cruel fact that took place recently in the estate of Le Ferriere of Conca, about 14 kilometers (8.6 mi) from Nettuno, is confirmed: such scenes and brutality are possible in real life. I'll get right to the scoop: The country bumpkin, Alessandro Serenelli, a young man of twenty years, stocky, with a low forehead and a scowl, lived with his father and mother [sic] in a house on an estate together with the family of a farmer, Goretti, comprised of his mother and his daughter Maria, a young girl of twelve years, pleasing in countenance and precociously developed. It took place at 2:00 p.m. yesterday while the sun was beating down on the fields. Alessandro was driving the oxen slowly, which was yoked to his plow. Maria was on the upper landing outside the farmhouse, humming as she mended the shirt of the young man who, in their common life working together, she considered a brother. The gaze of the young man, deep in the furrow, fell upon the jovial young girl, while flashes of unsatisfied desire passed before his sullen eyes. The bitterness of his youth aroused in him guilty thoughts and unmentionable cravings, while a strange stupor invaded the fiber of his being. He suddenly stopped the oxen and said to Maria's mother, who was helping him at work, "I have to go into the house for a moment—look after the oxen for me." The woman complied, and he walked away with his head lowered, reaching the farmhouse quickly. He climbed the stairs and went to the young girl, who welcomed him with a smile. He bent down to her and whispered obscene suggestions in her ear. "Come on, I want you," he said as he blew imperiously in her face. "Help!" cried the girl, terrified by the grim mien of the young man, and she tried to break free and escape. He covered her mouth with one hand, while he squeezed her strongly with the other and dragged her into the first room of the farmhouse. Meanwhile, her mother was unaware of what was going on, and she continued watching over the oxen while the gruesome scene was unfolding upstairs in that squalid room. Alessandro threw the poor, young girl down and attempted the supreme offense. Maria defended herself with indomitable courage from the assault of the filthy satyr. The views of nudity during that cruel struggle increasingly excited the perverse senses of the degenerate, who then felt the need to destroy and annihilate the object he had so desired and who rebelled against the satisfaction of his desires. He grabbed an awl with a fixed handle and began to pound the poor body with fierce blows. The sharp iron tore into and penetrated her young flesh; blood spurted from her open wounds, while the brute laughed idiotically as a sated beast. Her desperate cries for help were followed by the moans of the poor, frantic victim.

Tired from striking her, the bumpkin left the miserable young girl drenched in her blood and locked himself in another room. Two farmers, brothers Antonio and Domenico Cimarelli, came to the house. They heard the moans, and, becoming concerned, they climbed up the steps. They discovered poor Maria lying in a red pool of blood from her wounds, her eyes wide with terror, and unable to utter a word. They yelled for help. The mother and father [sic] of the poor victim did their best to resuscitate their unfortunate daughter. The authorities of Nettuno and Cisterna were alerted of the horrific deed. From Nettuno, the good brigadier Lorenzo Fantini and soldiers on horseback, Leonardo Ruggeri and Adolfo Pierottini, rode the distance of fourteen kilometers in thirty-five minutes. Shortly after, Doctor Bartoli and Stella dell'Italia public assistant, Lt. Giovanni Barbuto, both arrived. The police sergeant of Cisterna also came with more soldiers. The room where the brutal murderer had enclosed himself was opened. Everyone expected him to resist, but instead he allowed himself to be handcuffed, offering no resistance. He remained silent without saying a word, just as dark and sullen as when he had contemplated his victim atop the stairs from the field. Meanwhile, the Red Cross wagon stretcher came from the nearby estate of Carano, as did Lt. Baliva. With great care, the girl was transported to the hospital in Nettuno, where she arrived at about 8:00 p.m. Doctors Bartoli, Perotti, and Baliva operated by laparotomy because the blows of the awl had been purposely aimed at the abdomen. It was an unnecessary torment for the unfortunate girl who ceased to live today at 4:00 p.m. While interrogated, the brute admitted all the circumstances of the crime, as reported by us, and cynically stated that he killed her because the unfortunate young girl did not acquiesce to his wishes. That miserable wretch even cried like a baby throughout the night! When he boarded the train to be transported to Rome this morning at 11:00 a.m., menacing crowds shouted threats of death at the murderer as he passed by.

The Carabinieri had to protect him. Oh holy lynch law, how just you are in cases like this.

Il Popolo Romano, 8 July 1902
Third page, second column, bottom
Headline: *Horrible Murder*

Yesterday morning, the peasant Alessandro Serenelli, aged 20, arrived in Rome from Nettuno, escorted by the Carabinieri, who the other day, having suddenly entered the farmhouse called le Ferriere di Conca, fourteen kilometers from Nettuno, having failed to induce the fourteen-year-old peasant Maria Goretti to satisfy his bestial desires, killed her with blows from an awl. The horrible crime, needless to say, painfully shocked the populace of the countryside.

Il Giornale d'Italia, July 8, 1902
Third page, second column, center
Headline: *Grim Crime in Nettuno*

Maria Coretti, a nice peasant girl of just fourteen years of age, living with her family on Le Ferriere di Conca estate, fourteen kilometers from Nettuno, had aroused an ignoble passion in the peasant Alessandro Serenelli, twenty years old. The day before yesterday, he suddenly returned to the farmhouse and forcibly dragged the naive young girl into a room and attempted to insult her honor. Encountering fierce resistance, the brute armed himself with a sharp awl, hurled himself like a beast on the unfortunate woman, and peppered her with blows. Upon hearing the moans of the unfortunate creature, two peasants rushed [to her] and then immediately notified the Nettuno police. Alessandro Serenelli, who had locked himself in a room, was arrested. His victim was transported to the hospital, where she died a few hours later.

Il Messaggero, July 9, 1902
Second page, fourth column, bottom
Headline: *The Crime of Nettuno; Other Details*

On the little body of poor Maria Goretti, fourteen wounds were discovered, [resulting] from a dagger twenty centimeters long with a very sharp tip. The autopsy was performed by Dr. Bartoli in the presence of judicial authorities. Maria was known in Nettuno, where she often went with her mother to sell pigeons and fresh eggs. The poor girl, shortly before she entered the throes of death, told Dr. Bartoli that her murderer had made two other attempts on her virtue and had ordered her not to say anything, threatening her life. It was said that as soon as he was arrested, Serenelli made it known that his mother and brother had died of insanity. Due to the great precautions taken by Brigadier Faustini, upon departure for the prisons of Rome, the beast was not massacred by the populace, who were outraged by the brutal crime.

Il Messaggero, July 10, 1902
Second page, first column, bottom
Headline: *To Nettuno: The Funeral of the Murdered Girl—at the Sea!*
The funeral of poor Maria, the girl murdered by the peasant near Conca, was a true demonstration of regret for the victim and execration for the author of the horrible crime. Many participated, including a group of students with their teachers, clergy, and many members of the public. […] The archpriest spoke of the virtues of the poor martyr, which moved all those present. At the cemetery, over the earth that will cover the young girl's body, a marble monument will arise, which will be financed, with exquisite forethought, by the municipality, the archpriest, and a charitable foreign woman who assisted poor Maria in the hospital until she breathed her last breath.

22: Assunta and the Aftermath

After the tragedy, Assunta decided to return home to Corinaldo. The Gorettis were a tenacious, determined people, accustomed to standing firm in the face of difficulties. "God always provides," good Luigi used to say. His words were like a testament, or even viaticum, for the journey that was to be resumed. On November 2, 1902, Assunta set out on her return trip to Corinaldo.

In an unexpected surge of generosity, Count Mazzoleni paid for the Goretti family's trip from Conca to the Italian capital. He suggested that, once in Rome, they contact the police and request free repatriation for the remainder of the trip to Corinaldo due to "abject poverty." Assunta recalled, "We had nothing to eat. We spent three days and three nights in Rome in the train station. We slept on the floor on the bare pavement, without a blanket." [79] The station master took pity on their plight and provided them food.

Seven years after she left, now thirty-six years old, Assunta returned home. When she arrived in Corinaldo, everything was different. Though Assunta had an irrepressible inner strength, reintegrating proved to be more difficult than she had imagined. Not only was she poorer than before she left, the memories of her late husband and murdered daughter were burned indelibly in her heart. Gracefully, the people of her native city welcomed her and her children. The tragedy was well-known in her home town. Eventually, a gentleman named Antonio Montesi offered her and her children space to sleep in his shed.

Finding work also proved difficult. After reaching out to relatives and friends, she found employment first by Count Brunori, then by the Honorable Sandreani. Finally, the archpriest of Corinaldo, Don Marinelli, offered her a permanent job as his housekeeper. At this time, Assunta found more proper housing near the Church of San Francesco. In the meantime, Angelo, Alessandro, and Mariano began to find their first jobs.

Assunta's two daughters, Ersilia and Teresa, endured a different trajectory. The fact is that Assunta could not care for her five children. She was forced to put the girls in a home. With the help of Fr. Romolo Allegrini, the archpriest of San Rocco, he found a home for Ersilia and Teresa. The search even involved first Pope Leo XIII and then Pope Pius X. In October 1903, Ersilia was placed in an orphanage in Rome run by the Zoccolette sisters, while Teresa was taken in by the Franciscan Missionary Sisters of Mary. Years later, Teresa took vows in the same order.

During this period of precariousness, Marietta began to "make herself heard." Serenelli's trial, which was followed attentively by the press in Rome, also involved the Catholic press. However, they were sensitive to certain details concerning Maria's death that were not the purview of the secular press. They began to note characteristics of Christian martyrdom. On October 26, 1902, the weekly Catholic periodical *La Vera Roma* published news concerning the "Conca crime" on its front page and promoted a subscription for donations to build a monument to Maria.

Donations were surprisingly successful. A grassroots campaign sprang up, and donations arrived from all over Italy. The monument was realized by the sculptor Raffaele Zaccagnini and inaugurated in the Sanctuary of the Madonna delle Grazie (Our Lady of Graces) in Nettuno on July 10, 1904. A similar work was erected in Corinaldo on September 25, 1910.

Also in 1904, Carlo Marini, the editor of *La Vera Roma*, published the first biography of the future saint. Titled *Biographical Notes of Twelve-year-old Maria Goretti, Barbarously Stabbed to Death in Defense of Chastity*, it was dedicated to young men and women who "in the sweet spring of life and among the pestiferous mists of a corrupting age still keep the lily of innocence intact." In composing his work, Marini relied on firsthand sources. Thus, he handed down to us the first *Vita*, or biography, of Marietta. He wrote that she was:

> A little girl of beauty truly worthy of the brushstroke of Blessed Angelico. [She had] two marked eyelids, always

ready to veil her lively gaze with modesty, which highlighted the pale pink of her gentle face, which at the slightest occasion took on the sweet color of oriental sapphire. Her thick, blonde hair enhanced her charm. Her slender figure, endowed with artistic elegance, rendered her a flower of a girl admired by everyone. [80]

Marini's book went well beyond its noted literary style. It encapsulated a truth that was also emerging beyond the media scoop and making inroads in the world of faith. From here on, Maria Goretti was no longer confined to the crime beat of the newspapers. Her saga as a "little wildflower" became like a Passion narrative similar to the women martyrs from the early centuries of Christian Rome. In this context, Marini's tome could be considered prophetic.

By 1918, some of the early protagonists of the story had passed on. That year, Count Attilio Mazzoleni died suddenly of a heart attack in Rome. Giovanni Serenelli suffered the same fate. After the trial in Rome, he had returned to Torrette, where he was taken in by his grandson Costanzo, Pietro's son. He died there. Now, Assunta remained the most authentic witness of what happened.

On January 26, 1929, in the presence of Mamma Assunta and the Cimarelli wives, the remains of Maria Goretti were exhumed. On July 29 of the same year, in the presence of Assunta, her children Teresa and Mariano, the translation of Maria Goretti's relics took place. Maria's remains were interred in the famous Sanctuary of the Madonna delle Grazie in Nettuno. Initially, they were placed in the nave near the monument dedicated to her since 1904. Before returning to Corinaldo, Assunta expressed her gratitude to the Passionists for all they were doing for the glorification of her daughter, and she formally donated her daughter's body to their custody.

Meanwhile, Teresa and Ersilia, who had now grown up, returned to Corinaldo in 1918. In 1920, Teresa entered the Franciscan Missionary Sisters of Mary. Two years later, on June 29, 1922, Ersilia married. Teresa died on February 25, 1981, two years after the special meeting in Nettuno with Pope John Paul II, who came as a pilgrim to the sanctuary on September 10, 1979. Ersilia joined her on August 21, 1981.

Regarding the other Goretti siblings, Angelo and Alessandro both emigrated to America in the 1910s. Sadly, Alessandro died of pneumonia in America on January 10, 1917. He was only twenty-two years old. Angelo, on the other hand, lived a long life. Though he lived most of his life in the United States, he died in Italy in 1964 on a return trip to visit relatives. He was in his 70s. His remains were sent back to New Jersey, where he was buried. Mariano married Giulia Morbidelli in 1920 and died in Licola (near Naples) in 1975.

Assunta lived her final eleven years in the house of Ersilia. She died there on October 8, 1954, at the age of eighty-eight. Two years earlier, on the occasion of her daughter's fiftieth anniversary of martyrdom, she had received a personal letter from Pope Pius XII. Assunta Carlini-Goretti led an extraordinary life. Present at her daughter's canonization, she was referred to by the pope with the extraordinary title of "mother of a saint." Before her, only the mother of St. Luigi Gonzaga had such a privilege.

---

[79] Bruno Guerri, *Povera santa*, 144.
[80] Carlo Marini, *Maria Goretti*, (Roma: La Vera Roma, 1904), 15.

23: The Dream

While the Goretti family was seeking to rebuild their lives, Alessandro's agonizing odyssey through the Italian penal system was just beginning. Once the trial concluded and the sentence was handed down, the spotlight went out. Alessandro was whisked away from public view and sent to pay for his crime. Though Alessandro had fallen, he too would rise again. The new Alessandro would be reborn from the ashes of his past.

Alessandro spent the remainder of 1902 in Regina Coeli in Rome, waiting for formalities to be wrapped up and his fate to be decided. After Christmas Mass—which was (and still is) always a heartfelt moment in Regina Coeli—the warden called him to his office and told him where he was being sent. Alessandro would be interred in the notorious prison of Noto, in the province of Syracuse in eastern Sicily.

In February 1903, with his head shaved, wrists shackled, and vested in the traditional green-and-brown striped uniform, Alessandro began the journey south. He was guarded closely by two Carabinieri officers. They were alert to any sudden gestures he might make, as prisoners were often desperate in these circumstances. After arriving at Rome's Termini Station, he and the accompanying officers boarded a train and traveled south along the Tyrrhenian Sea, past Naples and Paola. In Reggio Calabria, they traveled by ferry across the strait to Messina in Sicily, then continued past Catania and Syracuse, arriving finally at Noto two days after having left Rome.

It was almost evening when the young man from the Marches in his early twenties arrived. In a meager bag, he had a patched shirt, a pair of breeches, and a horrible memory of his odious crime.

He looked terrified, as one would expect of someone whose world had totally collapsed. Surely, on the short jaunt from the train station up to the prison, Alessandro Serenelli did not have the time (or state of mind) to admire the sea or charm of Noto. With its churches and palaces, it was light years away from the mud huts of the "Planet of Mosquitoes" from whence he came.

In historic Noto, lore and legends abound. Lurking behind every church and bell tower, palaces and flowering gardens, there are stories. The ancient city had been inhabited as far back as the Bronze Age, though after a massive earthquake in 1693, the city was completely rebuilt anew in the Baroque style some eight kilometers (5 mi) away. Today a UNESCO World Heritage Site, Noto is considered the Baroque capital of Eastern Sicily.

In Via Garibaldi in the upper part of the city, however, the charm and lovely colors of Noto take a step back and give way to melancholy. Once a former convent dedicated to St. Thomas, in the nineteenth century, it became a drab, penitentiary prison. Driven by the southerly scirocco wind, a warm, light rain caressed the bars like a harp. This would be his dwelling place for the next thirty years.

After Alessandro was processed, he was issued number 3142. He would be referred to no longer by his baptism name but by a number. Then he was led down a dark, silent corridor to the isolation ward. No one spoke. Halfway down the passageway, the guards stopped. He was placed in cell number 186. The cell was narrow and made of rough stone with a small window at the top covered by bars. From the slight window, a biting, breathless sea breeze wafted in. Furnishings consisted of a cot, a plate, a tin jug, and a basket. Then the door was closed. He would remain here in silence and alone for the next three years. Alessandro recalled the chilling experience.

> Once I set foot in prison, they no longer called me Alessandro but 3142. This always remained my registration number. I felt like I was drowning into a nothing. I had become a number and nothing more. My sentence included three years of solitary confinement. Isolation is something that can drive people insane. Thank goodness it is now abolished, as there can be no greater punishment—always alone with your thoughts, always in silence. I had one hour

a day of walking alone in the courtyard. And there, too, I was always alone and always in silence. It'll make you go crazy, and many people did go crazy there. [81]

After twelve months of total isolation, Alessandro earned what was referred to as "half-word." With this privilege, prisoners were allowed to speak to each other in a hushed tone without being heard a half meter away. Perhaps now he was told how Noto was known for seismic activity. In January 1693, an earthquake razed the ancient city to the ground. However, it had long been rebuilt by the time he arrived. Perhaps Alessandro now understood that his actions on July 5 had destroyed the lives of so many people like an earthquake. And yet, like Noto, he, too, would be rebuilt. For nothing would be as before.

The turning point took place in a dream toward the end of this period. It was the beginning of his conversion. He described what happened.

> I was in my final year of that horrible solitary confinement. I thought I would eventually go insane due to so much suffering. Desperate thoughts—more and more violent—swirled in my mind. Then, one night, I had a dream. I saw myself before a garden, and there was a box full of white flowers and lilies. I saw Marietta come down, beautiful, dressed in white. As she picks up the lilies, she presents them to me and says, "Take them." Then she smiles at me like an angel. At her smile and benevolent gesture, without even thinking I should kneel down and ask her forgiveness for my ferocious crime, I was encouraged, and I accepted those lilies one by one until my arms were full. Soon, however, I realized that those lilies were turning into flames in my arms. Marietta smiled at me again and then disappeared. Startled, I woke up and thought to myself, "Now, I, too, am saved, for surely Marietta is praying for me. She came to visit me and give me her forgiveness." From that day onward, I no longer felt the horror of my life as before. [82]

---

[81] Ciomei, *Il Pugnale*, 41.

[82] Liberati, *Maria Goretti*, 107.

24: Life in Prison

After the three-year period of solitary confinement had passed, Alessandro's situation began to improve. He was now able to work, which kept him busy most of the day. Prison has its times and its rhythms. It is a type of self-sufficient village with its own rules and its traditions, to which one gradually becomes accustomed. He described a typical day.

> Around 7:00 a.m., after the alarm went off, they would bring me a sack of palm leaves to shred. The wooden comb they gave me was armed with twenty-seven iron teeth. The jailer counted the teeth three times a day. That's how it was. In that environment, some inmates often have bad ideas. During the long years I was in prison, I had various jobs and responsibilities that I tried to do in the best possible way. After the palm trees, I was put on laundry duty, which was washed twice a day with soap and washing soda. After two weeks, I became chief washer. I kept the register and received seventy cents a day instead of the ordinary sixty. One day when I was supervising the washermen, I said to them, "Make sure you wash a little better. I was called out by the warden because of you. Make sure he doesn't reproach me." At that, a bold Sicilian took a shirt soaked in water and threw it at me. My blood boiled, but I didn't react. By then, life had taught me something. From washerman, I advanced to the storeroom. There were many numbered boxes in the storeroom—one for each inmate. I had to put away the clothes, have them mended, deliver them, and register them. It wasn't hard work, but I soon lost my taste for it.

LIFE IN PRISON

Sedentary work wasn't for me. In the first eighteen years, I did all sorts of jobs: sweeper, janitor, chair repair. I also combed vegetable fiber, and I made matchboxes, for which they gave us twenty cents per 1,000. But I gladly worked as a form of release. The worst days were the ones when I had nothing to do. The warden once decided to let me learn the trade of carpenter, and he placed me as an apprentice in the workshop. But I didn't want to remain there. I felt suffocated and wanted to get out. Since he couldn't understand us, he bound me in irons. That was the only time I spent ten days "on the bed." In any case, I was used to the open air, and I couldn't stay put indoors. After the punishment, he listened to me. He was persuaded, and he sent me to work in the fields. The jailers were always "discreet," though the searches were a drag. They stripped everyone completely even in winter and searched everything, even loaves of bread. They searched us even at night, interrupting our sleep. I hardly ever cried. Only when I thought of my loved ones did tears come to my eyes. I didn't even curse or complain. I always had a closed character. "It's set now," I said to myself. "I just need to focus on getting out of here." The food was always the same slop, but we ate it anyway to survive. I never lost hope of getting out. We had only water to drink, except on Christmas or Easter when there was a quarter liter [1/2 pint] of wine. At our expense, we could purchase more than survival food—that is, bread and fruit—but never wine. I never received anything from anyone, except for my sister Lucia, the eldest of my siblings, who sent me a money order for five to ten lire and sometimes even twenty. She always wrote to me. This was my great and only comfort—regular and constant—that came from my relatives. Until his death (in 1918 at the age of eighty-one), my father always wrote to me every few months. His death was told to me by the chaplain. I was excused from work that day. My brother Vincenzo also wrote to me from America, though he never sent me anything. I felt remorse for my crime, and I had already confessed it while at

Regina Coeli. [83]

Alessandro recalled two figures fondly during his long stay in Noto. The first was the warden. His name was Corrado Rizzo Fiaccavento. Alessandro said of him:

> He was a heck of a man. He received us every day and listened to us patiently. He greeted everyone, had us sit down, and never sent us away without a word of comfort and giving us a loaf of bread—he always had two bags in his office for anyone going to their hearing. [84]

The other was Fr. Michele, the Chaplain. Alessandro said:

> He was particularly paternal, perhaps because he was older and was never in a hurry. He always listened to us and helped us in every way within the confines of the law. He gave us free objects of devotion and also tobacco for those who smoked. Before going to prison, I went to church, but I had never had direct contact with priests. In fact, I judged them with the current ideas of the times. In prison, I began to appreciate their extraordinarily mission of goodness. His word was always truly friendly and objective. [85]

During Alessandro's time in Noto, several historic events took place. In 1908, the Messina earthquake was felt all the way in Noto. Prisoners panicked due to cracks that appeared in the ceiling. There were attempts at mutiny, though Alessandro did not participate. Instead, he attended the religious service of thanksgiving for escape from danger, which was solemnly celebrated in the prison chapel.

During Italy's colonial war against Libya in 1911, fifty African prisoners of war were sent to the Noto prison, despite inevitable problems of coexistence. Then there was the so-called Great War (1915–1918). The warden announced it and invited the prisoners to contribute to the so-called National Victory Loan [that is, a series of government bonds issued by Italy to finance the war effort]. Alessandro signed over a 100-lire banknote with 5% interest. When he got out, he was given a check for 1,400 lire. He was given news of the [infamous Italian] retreat from Caporetto, as well as the victory on November 4, for which the imprisoned received a four-month commuted sentence. Amnesty for the twenty-fifth anniversary of the reign of Vittorio Emanuele III was much more substantial; on that day, each prisoner received a reduction in their sentence of one year.

In 1918, Alessandro was elevated to what was referred to as the "red class." When inmates had served half their sentence, they were given a red ribbon to attach to their uniforms. With the red ribbon, there were associated relaxations in the prison regime. Alessandro requested to be transferred to a penitentiary where he could work in agriculture.

"Send me to an agricultural penal colony," he said to the warden. However, he was told that since Italy was at war, transfers were dangerous. [86] All the same, Alessandro's return to his agricultural origins would take place sooner than expected.

---

[83] Ciomei, *Il Pugnale*, 47-8.
[84] Ibid., 42.
[85] Ibid.
[86] Ibid., 47-8.

25: Ongoing Conversion

Conversion involves an authentic change of life, moving from self-centeredness toward God. It is revealed in concrete gestures, and it inspires feelings that arise from a new heart. The path of conversion can accompany us throughout our lives (if we allow it to). It reveals visible fruits, ready to be harvested by the people close to us. However, it requires participation.

Even though Alessandro had the dream, there was the real risk of lukewarmness or backsliding by becoming too accustomed to the routine and drudgery of prison life. Alessandro's spiritual situation seemed gray, without any glimmer of light, even though the turning point had occurred. It was now a question of waiting on God and his times. Suddenly, things began to move.

Already by 1909, Serenelli had seen various articles and publications that not only recounted Maria Goretti's story but described her as a saint, in that she died "so as not to offend God." Alessandro said, "When I read that she had forgiven me before dying, it made such a great impression on me, to the point of tears." [87] Until that moment, Alessandro had remained in the dark regarding the "Goretti movement" that was now taking place throughout Italy.

In 1910, shortly after the erection of the monument to Maria Goretti in Corinaldo, Assunta took an initiative. She asked the parish priest of Corinaldo, Don Marinelli, to seek and find Alessandro. Assunta was determined to make contact with the murderer of her daughter and communicate her forgiveness to him. She knew that this was the right path to arrive at the definitive conversion of Alessandro. But no one knew where he was.

Don Marinelli went to the bishop of Senigallia, Mons. Cucchi, whose diocese included Corinaldo. He used contacts in Rome to discover Alessandro's location. Once Mons. Cucchi found out he was in Noto, he decided, in turn, to contact the bishop of Noto, Mons. Giovanni Blandini, asking him, in the words of Alessandro, "to come and visit me in prison, to check on my condition, to bring me some news, and encourage me to do good." [88] The bishop of Noto, though advanced in years, understood the importance of the matter and went in person to the former convent of San Tommaso in upper Noto.

Alessandro described that memorable day.

> I had never spoken face-to-face with a bishop. When they called me to the visiting room, I was full of awe. Soon, his fatherly manner came through and gave me courage. I don't know how to speak well, but I felt myself pouring out my heart to him. We discussed the "deed," and I told him everything, as best I could, including the "dream." The bishop dried his eyes with a handkerchief, but I was more moved than him, and I felt sorry for what I had done. Unfortunately, interviews are limited for prisoners, and our time was coming to an end. So, the bishop asked me if I had repented. "Of course," I replied. During sleepless nights, there are so many awful thoughts that someone would have to be totally depraved not to repent. Then, he told me to write a letter. "It would be my duty," I replied sincerely. But I added that I was not capable of writing [well]. But he insisted on writing freely, according to what my heart dictated. I did so, and I asked forgiveness from God, my victim's family, and society. He then blessed me with affection, and I think he invoked God and Marietta for me. Then, time was up, and we parted, saying goodbye. I would have liked that conversation that had become so intimate to last longer. As soon as he left the prison and arrived at his home, on November 10, 1910, the bishop of Noto immediately informed the bishop of Senigallia of the meeting he had with me and of the promise I had made to him about writing a letter. [89]

Alessandro returned to his cell with a heart overflowing with joy. He informed the prisoners of the conversation, and one of them agreed to help him draft the letter, though it "took place under [Alessandro's] dictation." Follows is the letter as Serenelli wrote it:

> To S[ir]. Exc[ellency]. Monsignor Bishop of the city of Noto.
>
> I cannot express what comfort my grieving soul received from the honor of having a conversation with Your Illustrious Excellency, for which I send you the warmest signs of thanks and gratitude.
>
> If it is true that in a moment of mental aberration I was compelled to commit such a barbarous murder, for which the law has already punished [me], I can never accuse myself that in doing so there was my firm and resolute will to cause so much harm. My young age and little knowledge of life were the initial causes that led me to the deed, which today I bitterly regret.
>
> I doubly regret the bad deed because I have the knowledge of having taken the life of a poor, innocent girl, who until the last moment, wished to maintain her honor, preferring to sacrifice herself rather than give in to my desires, which induced me to [commit] such a terrible and deplorable deed.
>
> I publicly detest [these] evil deeds, and I ask forgiveness from God and then from the poor, desolate family of the [girl I] murdered for the great crime I committed. I desire to hope that I, too, will be able to obtain forgiveness as many others of this land.
>
> To you, Most Reverend Excellency, I make this declaration in the hope that you will want to take it into account and you will want to forgive me, as I have done so much harm [due to my] inexperienced youth and that your prayers united with mine can give me the forgiveness of Him who rules all things and serenity and the blessing of the poor

deceased [Maria].

Respectfully kissing your hand and asking your most humble forgiveness.

Alessandro Serenelli
Noto Penitentiary
November 10, 1910 [90]

On November 13, the bishop of Noto sent Alessandro's letter to the bishop of Senigallia, who sent it in turn to Fr. Marinelli. He read it first to Assunta and then to the entire village during Mass. The emotion was great throughout Corinaldo. The archpriest, in a letter dated December 6, thanked the bishop of Noto on behalf of the village for the gesture made and, above all, because it had allowed contacts to be reestablished between the Goretti family and Alessandro Serenelli.

After this occasion, correspondence between Corinaldo and Noto became more frequent. Eventually, Alessandro was sent the biography of Maria Goretti, written by Carlo Marini, together with some editions of the *Vera Roma* publication, which reported on news of miracles and healings obtained through Marietta's intercession.

In 1911, war between Italy and Libya broke out and continued through the following year. Initial euphoria regarding Maria's cause diminished, given the complexity of the problems Italy was enduring. Worse, the winds of the Great War of 1915–1918 were blowing and menacing peace everywhere. In 1916, during the conflict, Alessandro was called to the visiting room again. A military chaplain wanted to speak to him. Alessandro was surprised given that he did not know the man.

With great amiability, the priest told him that he came from the front and that he had a beautiful story to recount. Maria Goretti had begun working miracles. He said that during battle, many soldiers had recommended themselves to the "Martyr of Le Ferriere" and were experiencing her intercession. He asked Alessandro if he trusted in the intercession of Marietta, to which Serenelli replied that every evening before going to sleep, he recited a Pater, an Ave, and a Requiem for her soul. Smiling, the chaplain replied that Marietta no longer needed to be recommended to God but that it was he who should recommend himself to her. As the priest went away, Alessandro felt serene. Serenelli wrote, "From that day, before going to bed, I prayed to Marietta with an Our Father and the Hail Mary, but I replaced the Requiem with a Gloria." [91]

Naturally, in the closed and gossipy prison environment, speculation about Alessandro abounded. The comings and goings of so many important personages did not go unnoticed. Some prisoners whispered of his imminent release. Others believed that his elaborate letter was merely a ploy to have his sentence reduced.

In reality, now that he had the red ribbon, Alessandro's time in Noto was coming to an end. He would not be liberated but transferred. The fifteen years in Noto had been very difficult, though graced by the dream, the rediscovery of a new Marietta, and contact with the bishop and Maria's family. Alessandro noted his conversion with amazement.

> The prison authorities, seeing my good behavior, considered transferring me to a healthier penal colony. Furthermore, partly due to my character, I didn't take part in occasional uprisings due to the terrible food. Nor did I ever attempt to escape, as others frequently did. Nor did I ever play card games. I did enjoy having my cards read because the fortune teller always promised me freedom in the short term. If you only knew how sweet the term freedom sounds in prison. [92]

Alessandro Serenelli's memory endures in Noto. To this day, the facility still serves as a maximum-security prison. However, the cell once occupied by Alessandro has now been converted into a place of prayer and dialogue for prisoners and chaplains. His story of being healed by forgiveness is an extraordinary sign of hope and trust for those who have none.

---

[87] Pujadas, *Yo maté*, 134.
[88] Ciomei, *Il Pugnale*, 43.
[89] Ibid., 43-4.

[90] Ibid., 44-5.
[91] Pujadas, *Yo maté*, 136.
[92] Ciomei, *Il Pugnale*, 48.

26: Toward Freedom

After receiving the red ribbon, in the summer of 1918, Alessandro received official notification that he was being transferred. He was sent to Augusta—still on the east coast of Sicily, not far from Noto. The penitentiary building stands tall on the north end of the island. In the penal colony here in Augusta, prisoners worked stones for the construction and expansion of the port. Though it was harsh work and wages were substandard, Augusta—with its medium level of security—it was a step forward from Noto.

The Augusta prison began as a Swabian castle in the thirteenth century. In the later sixteenth century, the Bourbon King Charles II expanded the castle with additional fortifications, transforming it into a powerful military fortress. Following Italian unification, the castle was reimagined as a prison. In 1978, the prison was disbanded.

Though the old prison once boasted mighty and impenetrable walls, it could not prevent the devastating global pandemic from entering the bars that year. In fact, shortly after Alessandro arrived in Augusta, he fell ill with the Spanish Flu. There was no medicine, and doctors sought to treat the symptoms. The influenza was responsible for tens of millions of deaths around the world, with as many as 400,000 in Italy alone.

Despite his suffering, Alessandro eventually saw his recovery in light of the particular mission that God entrusted to him.

> I caught the Spanish Flu in the Augusta prison in 1918. The doctor did nothing or almost nothing for me. I remember that the visit was quick, and he smoked the entire time. Looking back now, I see that it was the finger of God that kept me alive. The Spanish Flu was no joke. It

hit you mercilessly. It wiped out entire villages, and there was no space in the cemeteries even to bury the dead. But I see the finger of God regarding my situation, because if I had died at that time, I would not have been able to retract the slander I had leveled against Maria Goretti in court—slander that could have prevented her canonization. Whenever I think about this, I get goosebumps. The poor thing. She was as innocent as water, and my slander would have prevented her canonization. It would have been like killing her a second time. But God did not allow this, and he saved my life. [93]

Alessandro didn't stay in Augusta for long. Due to his poor health, combined with the esteem of the warden, he was transferred again. Less than ten months after he arrived, during Holy Week 1919, Alessandro Serenelli was transferred to another penal colony—this one in Sardinia, another Italian island in the Mediterranean.

The sprawling Mamone prison colony was located in the heart of the Barbagia—a vast mountainous region in the center of the island of Sardinia. Its main compound could accommodate up to 400 inmates, wardens, and housing for prison guards. There were five other branches: Sarcia, Nortiddi, Santissima Annunziata, Fiaccavento, and Temi. The entire complex was spread over 2,000 hectares (5,000 acres) among plateaus, woods, and slopes. It was situated in the territory of the municipality of Onani, although the most important city was Bitti. The terrain varied from 200 to 900 meters above sea level (650–2,950 ft), with cork, holm oak, and oak forests that opened up to valleys with very fertile land and five lakes. Halfway up the hill, prisoners cultivated fruit, citrus, and olives with a small oil mill and vegetables nearby. The "branches" were smaller prison complexes that could accommodate up to 100 inmates. They were essentially agricultural estates where prisoners were employed in farming.

Alessandro was initially sent to Nortiddi, 800 meters above sea level (2,620 ft), in the middle of the Buddusò plateau, not far from the Tirso springs. Though winters were harsh, the rest of the year was ideal. The air was good for Serenelli, and working outdoors felt like a return to his origins, for working the land was familiar to him.

Its rhythms and ways, consisting of sowing and harvesting, helped pass time more quickly. He described his transfer and the new prison reality.

> The time finally arrived to leave for the penal colony. We went by train to Livorno [in Tuscany], and from there we sailed to Sardinia. We disembarked at Porto Torres. From there, they took us past Sassari toward Bitti to the penal colony of Mamone, 600 meters above the sea (1,970 ft). The colony was fifteen kilometers (10 mi) from Bitti. There were several of them at the station; we were detached in number, about fifty, to Nortiddi, divided into three teams. We did all kinds of work in the countryside: deforestation in the winter, clearing in the spring, and sowing the wheat, which grew so high that it would lie down often. Vineyards were planted, and there was a vegetable garden for the house. We had many working oxen, a few spades, and many hoes. We reaped with scythes and threshed with oxen. The place was awful with precipices and ravines. There was little fruit and mostly wild. There were few religious services and Holy Mass, and the sacraments only a few times a year. [94]

On the "outside," Italy was undergoing another turbulent period. In October 1922, there was the Fascist march on Rome and the appointment of Mussolini as Prime Minister, followed by, two years later, the assassination of the socialist leader Giacomo Matteotti. There were also tensions within the Church and Italy's increasingly close ties with Hitler and Nazi Germany. While these events seemed light years away from that isolated corner of Sardinia, news penetrated the confines of the Mamone prison.

Alessandro recounted what evenings were like.

> In Bitti, I met a prisoner named Gabriele Alfonso, who was from Emilia Romagna. He couldn't stand the military life [which was compulsory then], so he deserted in Odessa. Then he traveled the world and engaged in thievery and other crimes. He was imprisoned in Messina [Sicily] at the time of the infamous earthquake. He used it as an opportunity to escape, and he filled a suitcase with stolen goods from the Corso. He later reached France,

> where he was nabbed by an agent in Marseille. He was tried for theft from unknown persons and convicted. He had a very adventurous life, and on winter evenings he spoke at length about his exploits. He made an impression on us, though we pitied him at the same time. In Nortiddi, I heard about Mussolini's Fascism and the Action Squads [also known as Black-shirts] for the first time. [95]

In 1924, Serenelli's detention in Barbagia came to an end. In all probability, since he was in his final years of his sentence, he was moved to a minimum security prison to help him reintegrate into society. Alessandro notes how it went.

> I was transferred to the penal establishment of Alghero, still in Sardinia—a beautiful town of Catalan origins. I was in the main compound for a while, but there was little to do. So I asked to be transferred to Cuguttu, a branch located between the road and the sea encompassing an area of 197 hectares (486 acres). There were about fifty of us. [96]

After passing along some mountain roads and inaccessible localities, he finally reached the Sea of Alghero. For Alessandro, it was the last stage on his long journey toward freedom.

The prison was located in the outskirts on the road to Sassari of the city. When he arrived, it was rural. He was interred in a branch called Cuguttu, which was an agricultural colony. He requested the transfer because he was averse to office work, which he had been assigned to in the main compound. In Cuguttu, he could work the land once again, which he preferred. Today, there is no trace of the former penal colony. Instead, there are residential houses. Alessandro left us his memories of his stay in Alghero.

> After some time, an "S" was placed on my arm. It stood for "unconsigned" [Ita: *sconsegnato*], which meant I was subject to less surveillance, and there was greater trust in my regard. I was summoned by the underboss Masala, who told me, "There is a job opening at the henhouse; if you behave well, you can work your whole time there. You can take some eggs, but don't get carried away and take any chickens." I'm not just saying this, but I behaved well. That was my last assignment as a prisoner. [97]

Testimonies attest that Serenelli did indeed behave well, which is the reason he received a reduction in his sentence. On March 7, 1929, he was summoned by the warden, who gave him the official news. His sentence had been remitted by an additional two years. In effect, he was free.

Alessandro was forty-seven years old when he was released. We have a photograph of him, taken with him in a new suit sent to him by his brother Pietro. His hair was thin, though his mien serene. He described how he felt that day.

> As God willed, my long period of incarceration had come to an end. Upon my release, I was congratulated by everyone. There was a celebration with soup, meat, and even wine. Freedom was so beautiful. I had longed for it so much, and it was worth it. I spent four days in the district prison, and on March 11, 1929, I left Alghero. I wore the new suit my brother sent me. The inmates bade me farewell, saying, "Go out like a gentleman." It was the moment I had looked forward to for twenty-seven years. I was finally free. [98]

When Alessandro left, he was given 1,400 lire—the interest on the 100 lire he had given to the National Victory Loan when he was in Noto at the beginning of the First World War.

The twenty-seven years of prison, which began when he was little more than an adolescent, marked Alessandro severely. The early years in Noto were hard on him, as was the Spanish Flu. His physique had changed so much that his sister and brother barely recognized him. A particular writer, using unbecoming language, described him as "a seventy-year-old who passed suddenly from an obtuse youth to precocious and idiotic senility. He is forty-seven but looks seventy: toothless, a few white hairs around a large bald spot, sunken eye sockets and cheeks, clumsy in his dress, old and formless." [99]

If his exterior had changed, his interior transformation was all the more profound, to the point that it was necessary to speak of a "new Alessandro." The dark tunnel he passed through after the "deed" he committed way back in 1902 in the Pontine Marshes could have led him in a different direction. He could have fallen into the abyss of no return. However, Alessandro chose the right path: that of redemption. The prison door that was shut after

Serenelli departed represented the end of a period of great suffering. It is also proof that if one wants to, he can be reborn.

---

[93] Ciomei, *Il Pugnale*, 49.
[94] Ibid., 49-50.
[95] Ibid., 50.
[96] Ibid.
[97] Ibid.
[98] Ibid., 51.
[99] Bruno Guerri, *Povera santa*, 163.

27: The Difficult Return Home

The country that Serenelli was reintroduced to had little in common with the Italian nation he had left behind at the beginning of the century. Politically, Benito Mussolini ruled Italy with an iron fist, especially after the Lateran Treaty reached with Pope Pius XI in 1929, which created the Vatican state and ended the suppression of the Catholic Church that had existed since unification. On the streets, there were no longer bicycles but cars, electric trams, and above all, giant portraits of *Il Duce*, that is, Mussolini. Radio and cinema had begun to eclipse the theater as the most popular form of entertainment, and new values were beginning to transform Italian customs and families.

The return to the site of his trial in Rome—and above all to Ancona—was not at all festive. The freedom earned by Alessandro would be granted gradually. Among other things, the first three years of freedom were limited by strict probation. This is how Alessandro described it.

> The return journey was not free but "forced." That is, I was not permitted to stop and see anything. We boarded a ship in Terranova (Olbia, Sardinia) and were in Civitavecchia (near Rome) on the morning of the 12th. I was then placed in the transit prisons back in Regina Coeli in Rome. On the 18th, still accompanied and handcuffed, I boarded the train to Ancona. At the police station, I was presented to the P.S. delegate, who asked me for my details. They asked me these things many times and in many places. He gave me the surveillance booklet and sent

me to the marshal, who gathered all the police officers and said to them, "This one is going to Torrette. Study his face carefully, and don't forget him. If you discover him out past hours, lock him up." They had already given me the little red booklet with the special surveillance regulations: Every Sunday I had to sign the booklet [in the presence of the officers], and I had free leave only between 5:00 a.m. and 8:00 p.m. I was not permitted to attend gatherings of more than three people, I could not walk on sidewalks, and I could not frequent public buildings, such as churches, cinemas, or shops. [100]

On March 21, Alessandro arrived in his childhood village of Torrette and was finally reintroduced to his brother Pietro. They barely recognized each other. There was a small welcome-home party, and Alessandro was acquainted with nephews and nieces who had been born in his absence.

Alessandro lived with his brother for two years, doing odd jobs and seeking more stable employment. However, the "special surveillance" he was subject to limited his possibilities. There were checks and signatures to be affixed to the booklet. Alessandro said that it "was unbearable for me, practically worse than prison. There was the illusion of freedom, but instead I was limited in terms of movement." [101]

Pietro suggested several times that Alessandro should consider marrying and starting a family, that is, lead a normal life. It would have been a way of settling with his past and a step towards reconciliation with "the other half of the sky." He introduced Alessandro to a woman named Valeria, who was a mutual acquaintance. But all such attempts in this direction were for naught. Alessandro was adamant.

> It was not on my mind at all. By then, I was accustomed to living a certain way. In the beginning, marriages are beautiful, but then comes pain. They proposed these possibilities, but I always thought it was too late. Moreover, I was afraid of creating a worse problem than the first. I received the last proposal some time ago, from people with the best intentions, but nothing ever came of it. [102]

Meanwhile, Alessandro's main concern was supporting himself, especially since he felt like a burden in his brother's house. The job applications he made in Torrette went unanswered. There were too many prejudices towards ex-convicts. He spent a few weeks in Colle Ameno working as a gardener's assistant, followed by a stint as a laborer with a construction company in Ancona. But his jobs never lasted long. His new life was a precarious and anonymous. It was one full of many hopes but few breaks.

Then, Maria Goretti "showed up" again, and Alessandro's life again took an unexpected turn. He talked about it.

> In November 1930, two women came looking for me. Armida Barelli from Milan and Jole Sampaolesi from Ancona—two important women with Catholic Action in Italy. They were quite interested in my conditions as a prisoner and in information about Maria Goretti, the reason I had been in prison. I had just gotten out, and I had fresh ideas to say to them. When they mentioned Maria Goretti, I felt a pang in my heart. Regarding prison, I said I had been sentenced to thirty years instead of life imprisonment because as I was a minor, and I got three years off for good behavior. I was nineteen when I committed the crime, blinded by my passion for Maria Goretti. I vividly described the punishments of solitary confinement and twenty-seven years in prison, so much so that, out of pity, one of them said to me, "Poor thing!" More moved than them, I added, "Well, certain crimes can never be paid enough." I thought of Maria Goretti. The thought of her moves me every time I think about her, and I continued. "Maria was truly an angel of a girl; she was innocent as water. She was so pious, so good, so helpful at home, a model girl." They wanted to know if what they had read was true, that at the moment of the murder, instead of blocking the blows to defend herself, Maria tried to cover herself while repeatedly saying to me, "Alessandro, you are committing a sin; you are going to go to Hell!" "Unfortunately, it's true," I responded sorrowfully. To comfort me, they reminded me that Maria, while dying, had said, "I have forgiven him. I will pray for him; Alessandro will be with me in Heaven." I understand

that my meeting with these two ladies of Catholic Action was later published in *Squilli di Resurrezione*, their weekly publication, in the November 1930 edition. [103]

The statements Alessandro made to Armida Barelli proved to be a key turning point. This was the first time he corrected what he had said during the trial in Rome in October 1902. After their conversation, Mrs. Armida Barelli decided to commit the prestige of the Women's Catholic Action to Maria Goretti's cause. It is no coincidence that in January 1935, Youth Week of Catholic Action took place at the Sanctuary of the Madonna delle Grazie in Nettuno, where Goretti's remains had been interred for six years. On the occasion, the Diocesan Council of Female Youth of Catholic Action of the Diocese of Albano, headed by Fr. Giuseppe Stella, promoted the canonization of Maria Goretti and asked Cardinal Granito Pignatelli of Belmonte to begin the Process.

Once the period of special surveillance was over, Alessandro could finally move about with greater freedom. First, he found a job in the countryside working for a gentleman named Mondaini, then with a Mr. Marconi, near the schools of Pinocchio, a hamlet of Ancona. He also worked for a landowner named Burattini, first in the old Valle Miano estate, then in Pietralacroce. But they were all seasonal jobs, and he was able to make a little money, nothing more. At the same time, the countryside was his world and the place where he did his best work.

On the other hand, there was no shortage of trouble. First, he had to contend with Mr. Burattini, who wanted him to sleep in a stable. Then he met a woman who made an indecent proposition to him. "She was florid and a bit fiery. If I hadn't had good judgment, there would have been trouble. As they say, 'when one has been pinched by the snake, he is also afraid of the lizard.'" [104]

In November 1930, his job search led to a Mr. Cesino Pesaresi, a landowner who had an estate near Aspio. It lasted briefly. Then, he spent the winter working for Enrico Osimani near the train station of Osimo. The cause of Alessandro's precarious work experiences was due to his past. He was the murderer of a martyr. Moreover, the reputation of Maria Goretti, especially after the release of the famous biography of Fr. Aurelio—which was translated into six languages—was becoming increasingly known.

Thus, when others learned he was her killer, he aroused "contradictory" reactions in people, to say the least.

At Christmas of the same year, Alessandro changed jobs yet again. This time, he would be working for a Mr. Vincenzo Buontempi. Finally, it was different. His latest employer told him, "We care little about your past. As long as you work and behave well, we won't have any problems." [105] Alessandro worked with Buontempi for four years.

Though the years following Alessandro's release from prison were a complicated and uncertain period and much more difficult than he had anticipated, for Alessandro, a season of hope lay just ahead.

---

[100] Ciomei, *Il Pugnale*, 52.
[101] Ibid.
[102] Ibid.
[103] Ibid., 53.
[104] Ibid., 55.
[105] Ibid., 57.

28: Christmas in Corinaldo

After the tragedy in Conca, as has been said, Mamma Assunta and Maria's sister Ersilia moved back home to Corinaldo. Aware that Alessandro was out of prison, Assunta sought to remove the "chestnuts from the fire," so to speak. Decades had passed since she uttered her cry of forgiveness in the courtroom of Rome. Life had not given her roses without thorns, and she had to struggle for her lot in life. And yet, with an entirely Christian sensitivity—always in line with Luigi's philosophy of life—Providence did provide.

Mamma Assunta asked the archpriest of Corinaldo, Fr. Bernacchia, in whose rectory she served, to take the initiative to invite Alessandro Serenelli to Corinaldo for Christmas. He was working in Osimo in that period, some fifty kilometers (32 mi) to the south. Shortly before Christmas, he received the letter from the priest, inviting him to spend the holiday with him. He also received money for the trip. "I accepted the invitation with an open heart," he said. "I knew that Assunta worked in the archpriest's rectory as his housekeeper, and I wanted to meet her face-to-face and ask her forgiveness for my crime." [106]

Early in the morning, in 1934, on Christmas Eve, Alessandro set out from Osimo. He took the train up to Senigallia and then boarded a bus to Corinaldo. Cloaked in frost and silence, an icy wind rushed in from the Adriatic Sea up the hills. All the same, he reveled in the beautiful countryside all around him.

Alessandro arrived in Corinaldo at dusk. With a heavy gait, he entered the old city gate known as Porta San Giovanni, climbed the steep Piaggia staircase, passed the Polenta well, crossed Via Cimarelli, climbed a few more steps, and finally reached Terreno Square. Before him was the Church of the Addolorata. He lowered his hat just above his eyes. Though it made it difficult to see, he wanted to protect himself from watchful eyes. Fr. Bernacchia's rectory was on the left. This was Alessandro's long-awaited moment. With his knees trembling, the last few steps seemed interminable. But there was no turning back. He summoned the courage and, with trembling hands, knocked on the door. After a few moments, Assunta opened the door. She gasped.

"Assunta! Do you recognize me? It's Alessandro Serenelli." Assunta looked at him in disbelief. She barely recognized the elderly man standing before him and gazed into his eyes for a long time. Finally, Fr. Bernacchia arrived and invited his guest to come in. Before the priest, between the door and the kitchen, Alessandro took off his hat, kneeled down, and said to Assunta, "I ask forgiveness, Assunta, for all the harm I did to your family."

Assunta stood there frozen. Finally, she exclaimed firmly, "God has forgiven you, my Marietta has forgiven you, and I forgive you." A long embrace sealed that extraordinary moment. Outside, in the sky above Corinaldo, the Christmas stars were coming out. The first footsteps of those going to midnight Mass could already be heard pattering along the road.

Alessandro described what happened next. "The next morning, we went to Mass and received Holy Communion together, united in the charity and forgiveness of God. I was happy. It seemed to me that I had rediscovered the affection of my poor mother on earth." [107] No one in Corinaldo spoke of anything else that Christmas.

---

[106] Ibid., 57.
[107] Liberati, *Maria Goretti*, 124.

29: It is my Duty to Tell the Truth

On November 7, 1935, Alessandro was at work in the fields when Mr. Bontempi summoned him. There were three priests who wished to speak to him. He narrated the encounter.

> The three priests were Fr. Alessandrini, our parish priest; the chaplain of Corinaldo, Fr. Camillo; and a Passionist priest named Fr. Aurelio. […] They pretended to be there by chance, passing through, but in reality they had come specifically to talk to me about Maria Goretti. They asked the owner if they could have some private time with me in a room, and they closed the door. After small talk, they told me that they knew the story of Maria Goretti from having read the biography, in which they also learned about my good behavior both in prison and on the outside, which made a good impression on them. They were words of comfort, but I must confess that when I recalled Maria Goretti, I had to take out a handkerchief and dry my eyes. "It's all my fault," I said at one point. I felt this deeply. The Passionist priest took out a small image of Maria, with his hand covering part of it so I couldn't see the name. He said, "It's a holy card of a contemporary saint. Do you know who she is?" "Of course I know her!" I exclaimed. He then told me that the little martyr would be declared a saint in time and that there was great enthusiasm towards her, even in the heart of the Holy Father. He then added that my word could be efficacious to this end. If I were to speak frankly, completely, and courageously, it could be an

appropriate reparation. "It is my duty," I interrupted. "I must make amends, and I must do everything in my power for her glorification. The wrong was all mine. I allowed myself to be blinded by brutal passion. And she was right to resist to maintain her innocence. She was truly innocent! In those days, young girls were not like they are now. They were simple and good, especially in the countryside. Maria was truly good. And to maintain her purity, she preferred to die under the hands of a murderer. So the blame was all mine." Then I added, "Now I just want to do everything in my power to contribute to the glorification of my victim." [...] The following month, at the beginning of December 1935, I was called to testify in the canonical process in Albano Laziale, where I disclosed everything in favor of her, who was innocent and who didn't even know evil. [108]

The wish of the Holy Father mentioned by Fr. Aurelio merits further clarification. He was referring to Pope Pius XI. Before being elected to the papacy on February 2, 1922, then Bishop Achille Ratti went to Nettuno to meet with Cardinal Pietro Gasparri, who was staying as a guest of the Passionists for a short period of rest. There, he learned of the story of Maria Goretti and visited the monument built in her honor. It made a great impression on him.

Some years later, Mons. Salotti, returning from Nettuno after the triumphal celebrations of July 29, 1929, in a private audience, expressed the desire of the people to see the promotion of the cause of her beatification, noting that she was killed in defense of her dignity.

Pope Pius XI replied, "Do you believe, Monsignor, that this is a true martyrdom?"

"Of course, Holy Father, since according to St. Thomas [Aquinas], even someone who dies to defend a Christian virtue is a true martyr."

"If this is the case, then we have Maria Goretti. Has nothing been done for her cause?"

"Nothing, Holy Father. It would depend on the Passionists, who safeguard her body in the Sanctuary of Our Lady of Graces in Nettuno. But due to their poverty, they can't even consider [the canonization of] their own religious, let alone the cause of Maria Goretti." [109]

The turning point, as we have mentioned, took place in January 1935, during the famous Youth Week. Cardinal Granito Pignattelli di Belmonte accepted the request, and Fr. Mauro Liberati—with experience in the cause of St. Gemma Galgani—was appointed postulator.

Fr. Aurelio's aforementioned meeting with Alessandro should be read in this context. By now, the circle was closing. For Marietta, the glory of the altars was becoming more and more probable.

---

[108] Liberati, *Maria Goretti*, 127.
[109] Mauro Liberati, *Una Storia Vissuta*, (Roma: Coletti, 1961), 40.

30: Alessandro's Mission

For Alessandro Serenelli, the time was approaching to lift up those "lilies of light" he received years earlier in the dream in Noto and to "proclaim on the housetops what you hear whispered" (Matthew 10:27). It is not easy for anyone to deny their past, especially if one's past involved innocent people. But in the light of the Word of God, Alessandro wanted to tell the truth, and it would be precisely that truth that would "make him truly free."

Thus, Alessandro decided to testify before the ecclesiastical tribunal as part of Maria's canonization process. The Information Process, which is usually held in the diocese where the Servant of God died, was begun in the bishop's palace in Albano on May 31, 1935. The solemn opening took place within a crowded room, full of joy that everyone felt in contributing to such a cause.

There was no conditioning or pressure that led him to testify, *sine glossa*, to the truthfulness of what occurred on July 5, 1902, in the Cascina Antica di Conca. Shortly before appearing before the judges, Fr. Mauro Liberati, the postulator, told him to "say what you know, for and against the Servant of God."

The eminent Cardinal Gennaro Granito Pignatelli di Belmonte, bishop of Albano, presided, flanked by numerous other prelates, clerics, and laypeople. The president took the floor and wished everyone to "work with seriousness and decorum." [110] Despite the arrival of a hot summer, everyone began to do so with professionalism and charity. Serenelli described how it went.

> From Rome, I went to Albano for the Information Process—a trial that wasn't intimidating despite the fact that it was full of judges and lawyers, including the "devil's advocate." A month later, in early December 1935, I was

called again to testify in the Sanctification Process in Albano Laziale, where I told everything in favor of Maria, who was innocent and didn't even know evil at all. [111]

He described Maria as "good, obedient, modest, religious, and innocent as water." He added that "I was the murderer who, blinded by passion, committed the horrendous crime. It was all my fault. I would be extremely fortunate if I could repair the harm done." [112]

The Information Process on the fame of martyrdom, miracles, and non-cult ended in 1935. The entire file was delivered to the Sacred Congregation of Rites, which analyzed the contents over the following two years. It was a meticulous and thorough analysis by the Vatican departments, down to the smallest details. Fr. Mauro Liberati recalls:

> Once the Process was delivered to the Sacred Congregation of Rites, the study began, which lasted about two years and led to the introduction of the Cause at the same Sacred Congregation. Of these, Cardinal Camillo Laurenti was then prefect. He was a man of God, a humble person, and quite fond of the Passionists. However, he died after the introduction of the Cause and was succeeded by Cardinal Carlo Salotti, who had served as Rapporteur and *ponente*. The Introduction decree was dated June 1, 1938, and Pope Pius XI signed the Introduction Commission with his own hand. Other things were completed in a short time, such as the confirmation of the sentence by Most Eminent Cardinal Pignatelli di Belmonte, bishop of Albano, regarding the "cult" never given to little Maria (July 7, 1938); the dispensation from the Apostolic Process on the fame of martyrdom in general; and that of the so-called Process called the *"diligentarium,"* because little Maria could neither read nor write. Thus the "remissorial letters" were obtained to begin the Apostolic Process on martyrdom, the Cause of the martyrdom, and on the miracles *in specie* of the Servant of God. This process began in September 1938. To the witnesses already examined and once again called to testify, seven more were added, all well informed. There were about thirty in all. [113]

Pope Pius XI, through the Cardinal Secretary of State, Eugenio Pacelli, in response to a telegram of best wishes sent by the Vicar General of the Diocese of Albano, said, "The Holy Father is losing no time, with vows and solemn joy, in the recognition of the angelic Goretti as a model for the protection of young souls." Interestingly, the canonical process went from May 31, 1935 until April 27, 1947, the day of the Solemn Beatification. It was just under twelve years, the length as Marietta's earthly life.

---

[110] Ciomei, *Il Pugnale*, 56.
[111] Mauro Liberati, *Una Storia Mai Raccontata*, (Roma: Coletti, 1961), 44.
[112] Liberati, *Una Storia Vissuta*, 44.
[113] Acts of the Apostolic Process, 118-41.

31: I Lied about Maria

We had the privilege of examining the document, *ACTS OF THE APOSTOLIC TRIAL ON THE FAME FOR HOLINESS, CAUSE OF MARTYROM, AND THE MIRACLES OF THE SERVANT OF GOD MARIA GORETTI*. Written in scholastic Latin, it felt like entering into the mystery of a great liturgy.

The pinnacle of the document is the moment when Alessandro took the oath, *Tunc praedicto testi iterum delatum fuit iuramentum, quod ille statum praestit genuflexus. Tacto pectore dicens*, "*Ita promitto et iuro. Sic me Deus adiuvet et haec Sancta eius Evangelia.*" ("Then the oath was again administered to the aforesaid witness [Alessandro Serenelli], which he took kneeling. Touching his chest, he said, 'I promise and swear. So may God help me and these Holy Gospels of his.'") His signature is equally moving: *Ego Alessandro Serenelli testis iuravi.* ("I, Alessandro Serenelli, a witness, have sworn.") Then there was an admonition, "The witness was warned of the sanctity of the oath, the secrecy to be observed, the penalties incurred, etc."

The first session began on October 8, 1938, at 3:30 p.m., with the Cardinal Bishop of Albano present, among others. Alessandro spoke on October 22 in the XII Session after Fr. Francesco Bernacchia, the archpriest of Corinaldo. This is Serenelli's deposition:

> I only testify to say things according to truth and justice, and I have not been pressured by anyone. I do not intend to exaggerate the virtues or silence the defects of the Servant of God. I desire her beatification, but I leave it to the judgment of the Church. I met her when my family lived together from 1898 to 1902. There were also her parents. I always found her to be good, docile, respectful,

and obedient with parents and with everyone. She was quiet and not grumpy by nature, and she was modest and reserved. When spoken to [by strangers], she was open and casual, though she never opened herself up much and continued on her way.

The session continued into the early afternoon.

Session XIII: October 22, 1939, 3:30 p.m.

After her father's death, she became an important source of support to her mother, more assiduous in prayer, and she said the Rosary with greater devotion. She was recollected in church and usually remained after Mass for a while. Once, in early 1902, she and I went alone to Mass in Nettuno. She was always honest, such that I never caught her in a lie. Personally, I have always loved work. I never took part in entertainment but preferred to stay at home and read. I have never been gruff or outgoing, and I liked to draw. Neither books nor newspapers had a [negative] influence on me. Regarding what has been said about me, regarding the walls of my room covered with illustrated newspapers, I was surprised [at what was said] because I simply enjoyed attaching a maximum of two or three figures, that is, a military scene, another of a thieving enterprise, and I don't remember what the third was. Two months before the crime, a bad passion developed in me towards her. I can say that cohabitation influenced the increase in passion towards the girl.

Session XV: October 25, 1938, 3:30 p.m.

With the excuse of getting a handkerchief, I went inside the house. It was July 5, 1902. I left with the determined desire to carry out what I had been planning in my mind for some time. [Editor: Since we have already recounted details of the attack elsewhere, we will omit those details here.]

Session XVI: October 26, 1938, 3:30 p.m. This was the key moment of the entire Apostolic Process. Here, the judges had the opportunity to ask for important clarifications.

I lifted Maria's clothes to repeat my temptation for the third time, but I was convinced in my soul that she would not allow it, and therefore I was more than prepared to kill her. Lifting her clothes, I realized that she was not going to give in; instead, she struggled and tried to escape. In an instant, I understood that there was nothing else to do but take revenge, and so I began to strike her. While I was lifting her clothes, Maria reproached me, saying, "God doesn't want these things to be done; you'll go to Hell!" And she repeated this phrase to me even as I struck her. She repeated it three times, then she did nothing else but shout and call out for her mother.

(QUESTION FROM ONE OF THE JUDGES): Is it true that at that moment, the Servant of God also said, "Yes, yes," as if to indicate that she was giving in to temptation?

(ALESSANDRO): After having thought for a long time about this, at this point, I declare that I remember that Maria said at that moment, "Yes, yes," but this expression of hers was preceded by the other, "God does not want these things, and you are going to Hell!" and was equally followed by the aforementioned phrase, "God doesn't want it and you will go to Hell!" And all the while, she was crying out and calling for her mother, and at the same time, she was struggling; and several times with her arms, she tried to pull up her clothes to cover herself. She never tried to stop my arm from hitting her but instead tried to pull up her clothes. Consequently, I can declare that I never had the suspicion, for an instant, that she was relenting from her opposition to my wishes. Her "yes, yes" in my way of thinking only serves to reinforce the other sentence, "God doesn't want these things; you're going to Hell!" I do not recall what Maria said when I grabbed her and dragged her from the landing of the stairs into the house. However, the correction that I make [now against] the accusation I made in the criminal trial [in Rome], in which I [hereby] declare that she firmly refused me, is given in good conscience. I also deny that I attacked Maria a second time. As if [as was said], when I let her be, she got up and went to the door to call for help, and I had chased her and struck her again to finish her off. [Instead,] my assault was only one, and I left her lying in a pool of blood.

(QUESTION FROM ONE OF THE JUDGES): How did Maria behave towards you in the timeframe between the second and the third temptations?

(ALESSANDRO): I noticed it then, and I still recall today that the Servant of God, despite finding herself forced by the necessity to work or remain in my proximity, always tried to stay away from me. And while before my temptations, she was more open and simple with me, after the first temptation and much more after the second, she had a more reserved demeanor, so much so that she avoided even looking at me. However, she remained docile and obedient when I asked her to do something for me. [...] At the time of the crime, I was not drunk, though I had drunk a little wine, or rather watered-down wine. I was not even fazed by the sun. Instead, I had the understanding that I was carrying out an action that was condemned by God and that I invited the girl to participate in my sin against the law of God.

Session XVII: October 26, 1938, 8:00 a.m.

After the crime was done, I locked myself in my room, and shortly thereafter I realized that some people had come up to the house, and I could distinguish the voices of my father, Assunta Goretti, and Teresa Cimarelli. No one told me what the Servant of God said to them. I don't know anything about the rest of the questioning [involving Maria], because I suppose that she was taken to her mother's room, where she had a cot, and from my room, it was difficult to hear what was said in her room because there were two other rooms between hers and mine, that is, the kitchen and my father's room. I threw myself on the bed but was tormented by remorse. I was arrested by the Carabinieri, who came from Cisterna. These officers handcuffed me and took me from my room down the steps, and we waited in front of the stable for the

Carabinieri to come from Nettuno because they knew that they, too, had been alerted. In fact, those officers came, and I was handed over to them, who transported me to Nettuno. They were on horseback, and I was walking between them at an accelerated pace but not running. Along the way, we passed the marshal who was coming from Nettuno. After counseling his soldiers, he was on his way to Le Ferriere di Conca for an inspection. Likewise, along the road, the ambulance coming from Nettuno passed us headed toward Le Ferriere, and the same ambulance passed me again when I was almost at Nettuno. The officers said that the ambulance was carrying the injured Servant of God. From the documents of the criminal trial, I know that the Servant of God died the following day. I don't know anything about the rest. I repeat, the only reason why I attacked Maria and killed her was the one I have already explained; that is, that she did not wish to consent the previous two times to my desire to carry out unvirtuous acts. I said and I say again that the third time, I tried to repeat the unvirtuous act, and I lifted her clothes, but since I saw that she continued opposing me, I immediately began to strike her. In my mind, there was no other reason than revenge, because she had refused me, and I understood that the unvirtuous act to which I invited her was against the law of God. I believe that the Servant of God understood that that act to which I invited her was against the law of God. I deduce this from her way of life and from the diligence with which she took care of her younger siblings. Furthermore, I deduce it from the very words she addressed to me at that moment when I lifted her clothes, "God doesn't want these things; you're going to Hell." In my opinion, it seems clear that the Servant of God opposed me not only out of a natural sense of modesty but by God's prohibition. During the time that passed from the first to the final temptation, I noticed that Maria prayed more than usual. I noticed this even though I was overtaken by my passion. I would add that I was not thinking of marrying Maria at all, just as I was not moved to kill her out of spite or revenge for family affairs but only out of my passion. The response that I gave to the investigating judge, Mr. F. Basso, at the criminal trial that is contested against me does not correspond to the truth, because the truth is what I have testified before this ecclesiastical tribunal in the various sessions held so far as well as before the ecclesiastical tribunal here in Albano a few years ago. I equally retract, as untrue, that I hurt Goretti because she had rejected my proposal of love and that I, at the moment of wounding her, did not understand what I was doing, as it reads in the Carabinieri report. My proposal was for unvirtuous acts, as I said above, and I killed her because she refused to consent to my propositions. And as much as I was overcome by passion, I understood what she was doing. Equally false is what we read in the acts of the criminal trial and especially in the medical report, that I killed the Servant of God in order to be supported [materially] by the government. I equally contradict what is read in the medical report regarding the expression, "yes, yes," uttered by the Servant of God. As I have already said repeatedly, the Servant of God uttered "yes, yes," preceding and following the other phrase, "God doesn't want these things; you're going to Hell!" I never remotely thought that her "yes, yes" meant consent to my desires. I would like to correct yet again that the first temptation was not one year prior, but one month prior [to the attack]. I confirm that from her first refusal, I felt resentment towards her because I was displeased that she would not give her consent. It is still true that a couple of times in that last month when I saw Maria, I felt excited with lust. However, she had done nothing to entice me with such a motive. In conclusion, everything I said in the criminal trial that contrasts with what I have testified here is untrue. The truth is what I said before this ecclesiastical tribunal. My thought is that the Servant of God died in defense of her purity.

Ego Alessandro Serenelli testis deposui ut supra. (I, Alessandro Serenelli a witness, have testified to the above.)

With that, Alessandro's entire defense in the Rome criminal trial held in October 1902, in which he said that Maria Goretti had given her consent and that the murder occurred only so that he would go to prison and be supported by the government, was retracted. It should be noted that the judges in the Roman penal trial did not believe his false testimony and condemned Serenelli all the same. Without the resolution of these key points, however, the apostolic canonization process would have ended.

Alessandro slipped out of the limelight just as quietly as he had entered. Yet he would still have another thirty years to tell the world about Marietta, always with discretion and humility. But now his mission was concluded. The danger of "killing her a second time" had been thwarted. He could now return to the shadows.

32: Saint Maria Goretti

1939 was a year of fear and foreboding. The two great ideologies of the century—Communism and Nazism—were filling gulags and concentration camps alike with blood and horror. On February 10, 1939, Pope Pius XI died suddenly, leaving his encyclical *Mit Brennender Sorge* (With Burning Sorrow), in which he condemned Nazism, incomplete. On March 2, Cardinal Eugenio Pacelli ascended to the papal throne, taking the name Pope Pius XII.

These events profoundly marked the life of the Church. On September 1, 1939, Germany invaded Poland, triggering the beginning of the Second World War. The war—considered the bloodiest in the history of humanity—led to an estimated 50 to 85 million fatalities. Italy experienced the war dramatically. There was the rise of Fascism and Italy's alliance with Hitler, the Allied landings in the South, the overthrow and execution of Mussolini, and the long period of reconstruction. Rome itself was not spared. After the bombing of the historic Basilica of San Lorenzo (St. Lawrence), images of Pope Pius XII visiting the famed church in the aftermath were seared into the memory of the faithful.

With these events in mind, the ten years that passed between the conclusion of the canonization process and the beatification of Maria Goretti can be better understood. The war shook the Church at every level. Moreover, unexpected difficulties arose due to irregularities that were discovered in the various procedures.

These moments of bewilderment and confusion were summarized by Father Mauro, who said to Mamma Assunta, "We need to pray much, because the devil is envious of our work and is trying to ruin it." [114] In another writing, the same priest and postulator of Maria's cause noted,

> There is no need to explain (the delay). But it is not without merit to say that there are third parties involved in well-thought-out and seriously considered works. If these people do not ruin the opus, they are at least a cause of disgust and bitterness. And how much bitterness had to be suffered in the cause of Marietta. [115]

The dispute concerned a signature that was missing from the court documents. In the XV Session on October 25, 1938, Fr. Alfredo Liberati neglected to sign several papers. Therefore, on November 19, 1940, the Sacred Congregation canceled the entire Apostolic Process that had taken place in Albano and everything had to be redone—with all the consequential problems. The new process, referred to as the Additional Roman Apostolic Process, was held from February 6 to April 3, 1941, in the headquarters of the same Sacred Congregation of the Rites before the same Promoter of the Faith. Alessandro Serenelli came again to testify. He confirmed his previous testimony.

The positive aspect of this event demonstrates the transparency and prudence with which the stages of the path towards beatification were marked. Among the most debated topics was that of martyrdom, which involved the respective Vatican departments from October 1942 until the General Congregation in the presence of the Holy Father in January 1945.

Despite the meticulousness of the investigations, before making his decision, on March 25, 1945, the pope summoned Cardinal Salotti and Bishop Natucci, Secretary of the Congregation, for further discernment. Finally, Pope Pius XII signed the declaration, which left no doubt. After an in-depth examination, "the martyrdom of the Servant of God Maria Goretti was established." The declaration cited a canon from the 1917 Code of Canon Law, which notes that for the "cause in question, a miracle is not necessary."

Before the closing of the Apostolic Process, as prescribed, the canonical recognition of Maria Goretti's body was carried out. It was a touching moment that we leave to the pen of Father Mauro Liberati.

> The urn was removed from the place where it had been walled up ten years earlier and was brought to the sacristy

of the Sanctuary [of Our Lady of Graces] in Nettuno. There, in the presence of Monsignor Salvatore Natucci, the general promoter of the faith; Monsignor Giovanni Calui, the chancellor of rites; two doctors; and others necessary for the ceremony, the bones were removed from the closed box in the urn and reassembled on a small table covered with a white sheet. The two doctors recomposed the skeleton by numbering the bones. They declared that Maria Goretti measured in height between 140 and 150 centimeters (4'7" and 4'11"). Therefore, she was quite developed, though not quite twelve years of age. The bones were then enclosed in a new wooden and zinc box and sealed with the [episcopal] seal of Monsignor Natucci and then walled up in a small niche dug into the wall next to the monument to the Martyr, inside the sanctuary, where they remained until 1943. During the war, in order to avoid danger and destruction, with the permission of the Sacred Congregation of Rites, on December 3, 1943, Marietta's remains, together with the statue of the Our Lady of Graces, were kept in the Generalate House of the Passionists of Sts. John and Paul at the Celio [in Rome]. [116]

Pope Pius XII signed the Decree of Beatification on May 21, 1945. But due to the conflicts, the ceremony took place on April 27, 1947, the third Sunday after Easter. With an overflowing crowd, there was additional excitement due to a unique fact: the mother of the newly declared Blessed was present, together with Maria's siblings Ersilia, Teresa, Mariano, and Angelo. Maria's other brother, Alessandro, had died on January 10, 1917, at the age of twenty-two, in America where he had immigrated. Alessandro Serenelli was not in Rome, although some in the media reported (falsely) that he was present, disguised as a friar, complete with a habit, long beard, and sandals.

There was a historic and extraordinary meeting between Mamma Assunta and Pope Pius XII. After embracing her, he told her, "How fortunate you are to be the mother of such a daughter, a saint." [117]

Among the numerous miracles attributed to the intercession of Blessed Maria Goretti, two were chosen for Maria's canonization, which took place on June 24, 1950. Due to the huge crowd, Pope Pius XII decided to celebrate the event in St. Peter's Square. Newspapers around the world described a memorable morning, with another photo of Mamma Assunta following the ceremony.

Alessandro Serenelli did not go to Rome. He described that day and the reasons for his absence.

> In April 1947, there was the celebration of the Beatification in Rome. It was a celebration for me, too. By now, I was sure I had a Protectress in Heaven. One day, a helper [in the Capuchin convent] said to me, "I read that they invited many people for the celebration in Rome. Are you going?" I said I didn't think it would be proper. After the canonization, solemn celebrations were also held in Corinaldo, the birthplace of the Blessed. I went there privately and prayed for a long time before her holy relics, and then I went to Assunta. But I did not go [to Rome] on the day of Marietta's beatification, because I would have been pointed out. Here, too, I go to Mass in the friars' choir [instead of in the public church] for the same reason. [118]

Regardless of the dates and circumstances, it is understandable how Alessandro Serenelli would have felt regarding Maria's beatification and canonization. His role as the "murderer of a Saint" is not unique. However, the fact that he lived throughout the Canonical Processes—and contributed to her canonization with his testimony—is unique in the history of the Church. Yet prejudices and hostility would continue to accompany him throughout his life, and he would have to work for his daily bread until the end. All the same, his spiritual life had certainly matured, summed up in that phrase he often repeated, "For the evil I have done, what I have to suffer is little." [119]

---

[114] Giordano Stella, *Il martirio di S. Maria Goretti*, (Pasian di Prato: Campanotto Rifili, 2002), 98.
[115] Liberati, *Una Storia Vissuta*, 45.
[116] Liberati, *Maria Goretti*, 132.
[117] Ciomei, *Il Pugnale*, 64.
[118] Ibid., 72.

[119] Liberati, *Una Storia Vissuta*, 76.

33: Return to the Cascina Antica

The Goretti and Serenelli families moved into the Cascina Antica farmhouse in February 1899. After the attack on July 5, 1902, in November of that same year, Giovanni Serenelli, Assunta and her children, and the Cimarelli families were evicted by Count Attilio Mazzoleni. Like his other farmhouses, the Cascina Antica was then rented to other laborers who came to work on the vast Conca estate. In a yellowed photograph of the Cascina Antica, dated 1920, on the ground floor, there is a sign for a "flask shop." The windows are bricked up, the roof is crumbling, and the rest of the house is deteriorating.

The project to restore the two farmhouses—the Cascina Antica and the one nearby where the Cimarelli family lived—was the initiative of Fr. Mauro Liberati. The more Maria's Canonization Process progressed, the more he realized the importance of preserving the site of her attack. There was the real risk that as time wore on, it would be more and more difficult to claim it as a site of worship and prayer. Moreover, negotiations were not easy, especially due to the high asking price of the owner.

Eventually, Fr. Mauro managed to have a plaque attached to the façade of the farmhouse, acknowledging it as the scene of the tragic attack. It was affixed on October 3, 1941. For the occasion, Assunta, her children Ersilia and Mariano, and the Cimarellis all came from Corinaldo. It was the first time any of them had been back to the Cascina Antica.

Fr. Mauro was also present. He said that "Assunta cried inconsolably, and in that circumstance, when asked for information on the precise place of the martyrdom, Assunta was unable to give it, since the house had been completely transformed." [120]

Once the long Beatification Process was concluded, Fr. Mauro decided to go ahead with the purchase of the Cascina Antica, including the land worked by the families. The biggest difficulties were due to the owner of the property, a gentleman named Libero Urbani, who lived in Rome. He had installed an electric mill for cereals in the farmhouse where the Cimarellis had lived, and this was his principal source of income. He didn't intend to give it up unless he could earn enough to build another one.

Urbani asked for 6 million lire (estimated at $100,000 USD today). This was an incredible amount of money, well beyond the resources of Fr. Mauro. After two years passed and the canonization in St. Peter's had concluded, Maria Goretti's name became famous throughout the world. Inevitably, everything related to her had acquired an extraordinary "inflationary" value. At that point, the Passionists of the Roman Province, to avoid further speculation, purchased the two farmhouses for the sum of 26 million lire (estimated at $433,000 USD today).

Then a project was launched to convert the Cascina Antica into a place of worship. The farmhouse inhabited by the Cimarellis would be dedicated to social projects entrusted to the Passionist Sisters. In 1952, restoration work began with the aim of restoring the buildings to their original design and repairing any damage caused by neglect and the war. Much credit goes to Cardinal Francis Spellman, archbishop of New York and titular of the Basilica of Sts. Giovanni and Paolo in Rome. He was a great friend of the Passionists and was also particularly devoted to St. Maria Goretti. The works were completed in 1988 and were signed by the Passionist architect Fr. Ottaviano D'Egidio.

Another difficulty that needed to be resolved was determining the exact spot where Serenelli attacked Maria. The early biographies referred to the kitchen, but it was not clear where it was due to numerous modifications to the house over time. Only Alessandro could resolve the question. Father Mauro gives important context.

> When I began to visit the farmhouse, there were two families living there. One lived in the room immediately after you entered, while the other, who had custody of the

entire building, lived on the left side where the Gorettis had lived and had the large room where the hearth was. Some people thought that the attack had taken place there, and they also took photographs complete with a sign to draw the visitor's attention. But this couldn't have been the case, as it did not correspond to clues that were found here and there. Wishing to know with certainty something so important, I wrote to the Father Guardian of the Capuchin friars of Ascoli Piceno, where Serenelli was staying, asking if the latter could come to Rome for a matter of such great interest. Serenelli came, was lodged at the Scala Santa, and the following day, we went together to Le Ferriere. It was December 16, 1950. Once we arrived on site, I told him the reason why we had gone there—that is, to know from him the exact site where the painful event took place. After climbing the external staircase and entering the door that leads into the house, Serenelli bent over and touched the floor with his hand. Trembling, he said to me, "I killed her here." I didn't say a word. Two large tears fell from my eyes. Witnessing the great agitation aroused within Serenelli's soul in seeing the place of his crime after almost fifty years, I spoke of something else, and we left. [121]

Alessandro also recounts this particular moment.

[Fr. Mauro] took me to the house in Le Ferriere where "the deed" took place. It was the only time I ever returned. Without explaining myself, I want to express the turmoil of my mind, of the blood of my heartbeats in approaching and returning to that house, which I tried not to show outwardly. Once I set foot inside, I leaned against the interior door jamb, trying to demonstrate a certain ease or fortitude (you know how men are.) But in reality, I felt myself falling over from the internal turmoil. [Father] asked me to show him the precise spot. "I killed her here." And with my hand, I pointed to the spot just inside and in front of the door. Later, they told me that they had placed a marble plaque there with a bronze statue of Maria Goretti, mortally wounded and fallen to the ground there. [122]

Today, there is indeed a bronze bas-relief on the floor just inside the main door leading to the kitchen. It was initially offered to Fr. Mauro for 200,000 lire, but at that time there were other expenses needed for the beatification. A few years later, Fr. Mauro happened to come across the same bas-relief, which was being kept in the Vatican.

"If I had the money, I would buy it," the priest said to Comm. Seganti, head of the Floristry. Seganti looked at him with surprise and suggested making the small request to the Holy Father himself, who would certainly donate the money. The request was made, and after a few days the answer was affirmative.

Fr. Mauro went to the Vatican, picked up the bas-relief and affixed it on the floor of the Cascina Antica at the exact spot indicated by Alessandro. That site is currently the most venerated place in the Cascina Antica. It is always adorned with flowers, and the saint's face is worn due to the many caresses of the pilgrims.

---

[120] Liberati, *Una Storia Vissuta*, 79-80.
[121] Ciomei, *Il Pugnale*, 58-9.
[122] Pujadas, *Yo maté*, 158.

34: Towards the Convent

Parallel to his spiritual journey, Alessandro experienced a human one of ups and downs. The fact is that his designation as the "murderer of a saint" followed him until death. Despite his tenacity and good will, the ghosts of his past continued to haunt him. Serenelli described it.

> In Corinaldo, I didn't experience any dirty looks, and only a few reminded me that I was the murderer. Assunta, in fact, took a strong interest in ensuring that her relatives would also forgive me. But for various reasons, some refused. This caused me much grief, but I understood that Mamma Assunta's pain was no less than mine. [123]

There is another episode in which Alessandro asked for forgiveness from Mariano Goretti, who at the time was married and had five children. After a while, Maria's brother said, "Yes, I forgive you. But what you did certainly wasn't a good thing." [124]

Alessandro's fame grew in proportion to Maria's. While she was becoming famous, he was becoming more and more infamous. As the hostility and prejudice grew around him, Alessandro became slowly convinced that "the world" was not for him. He came to desire a quiet and peaceful place that was secluded and far from everyone and everything. In such a place, he could lead his life with dignity. However, Alessandro Serenelli was in his early fifties. His age, plus his past, meant he would never have been able to enter a religious order. On the other hand, every convent had a vegetable garden to look after and countless projects to be done. Surely there was a place for him.

In 1936, Alessandro fell seriously ill with bronchopneumonia. After the difficult recovery, he felt as if his age doubled,. He recounted the experience.

> God allowed me to have a period of isolation due to bronchopneumonia, for which I was hospitalized. The religious there treated me with love and veneration. Meanwhile, the archpriest of Corinaldo was trying to help me find a different [living] solution. On various occasions, I mentioned to him my desire to move away from San Biagio in Osimo and cease to have contact with the world, and that in the solitude of a convent, I could experience love and peace and live a life of purification, where I would be protected from the morbid and offensive curiosity of the people. [125]

At the end of 1936, Alessandro went to Corinaldo to speak with Fr. Bernacchia, the archpriest. He asked him to help him find a "little place," given that he could no longer do the hard work in the countryside. Providence took the form of a Capuchin priest named Fr. Luigi da Monterado. He took the matter to heart and also dedicated himself to helping Alessandro.

A few months later, together with the archpriest, Alessandro was invited to the Sanctuary of Ambro in the foothills of Mt. Priora, part of the Sybilline Mountains. Here the aforementioned Capuchin priest lived. Alessandro immediately fell in love with the place, as the sanctuary embodied everything that he desired. After a few days, Fr. Luigi sent him the money for the trip (twenty-two lire), and he moved his belongings to the Capuchin friary in Ambro.

The Sanctuary of Our Lady of the Ambro takes its name from the Ambro River that flows nearby. It is one of the oldest and most visited sanctuaries in the Marches, that is, after the Holy House of Loreto. At a height of 658 meters (2,160 ft) above sea level, nestled between Mount Priora and Mount Castel Manardo, it offers extraordinary vistas of the surrounding mountains and landscape.

Referred to as the "Little Lourdes of the Sibylline Mountains," the sanctuary is due to a Marian apparition. Our Lady appeared here to a little girl named Santina who had been deaf and mute since birth. In exchange for the prayers and offerings of flowers that the girl would bring to an image of Our Lady placed in the cavity of a beech tree, the Holy Virgin gave her the gift of speech.

A few kilometers away from the Ambro Sanctuary is the village of Amandola. Here, there is another Capuchin friary. During the summer months, the Capuchins from Amandola would relocate to Ambro and then return in November. The Capuchin convent is situated up the hill, not far from Amandola. Alessandro spent time here, too.

"I always got along well with Fr. Luigi da Monterado. So when he was transferred to the convent of Amandola, though not as superior, I preferred to follow him. So I went there." [126] This was a peaceful period for Alessandro. Fr. Luigi was like a protector to him—a true moral and spiritual support. In Amandola, Alessandro was entrusted with cultivating the vegetable garden, a work congenial to him. He seems to have found the peace he was looking for.

However, a truly unpleasant episode occurred. He described the event.

> There was a hired hand in the convent, an elderly man named Mugnetto. He often got drunk, and due to some misdeed or another, he was fired. In order to stay on, despite everything, he devised a strategy. He pretended to have been robbed of his savings that he hid in the store: 4,000 lire. It was July 11, a Sunday. The Carabinieri were called, and they interrogated me and a young man named Troiani. We were both suspects. The sergeant told us, "You know where the Carabinieri station is located. Go down there and have them put you away." I showed up at the barracks first. The jailer was amazed and observed, "It is not easy for someone to show up spontaneously in these barracks." Since I had been in prison, there was a lot of suspicion about me. The marshal was good, but he didn't believe my protestations of innocence. He continually told me, "Alessandro, just confess! I won't even report you. I don't want any more trouble to happen to you, also because up until now you've always been on good behavior. Confess and return the money, and I promise to set you free." But I had nothing to confess! Those fifteen days were a martyrdom. I hoped that my innocence would triumph in the end. Even Fr. Luigi testified well about me. But what can you say? With my past, no one believed me. I

prayed to Marietta. Then, one day, there was another search, and the infamous 4,000 lire were found well hidden. The other gardener was arrested, and he confessed. Then I was immediately set free. From that day on, I never had anything to do with the law again. As soon as I returned to the convent, however, the superior, Fr. Raffaele da Cingoli, said to me, "After what happened, I can't keep you here any longer. You'll need to find another place to stay." [127]

Certainly, it would be easy to imagine Serenelli's state of mind. The ghosts of his past were always ready to haunt him even more than before. Yet God was at work. Though Alessandro's experience in Ambro lasted as little as a few months, it was significant. It represented a clean break from the world, which had been so harsh. But his motives were also existential: prison had played a part, work represented his survival, and there was a need for total recovery, beginning with spirituality. Lastly, he always had a desire to repair the damage done. He said, "The convent—secluded from the world, with its silent corridors, the church—has been for me during these long years like an oasis for the thirsty, a refuge for the sailor." [128]

---

[123] Pujadas, *Yo maté*, 158.
[124] Ibid.
[125] Celestino Nerone. *L'uccisore di S. Maria Goretti*, (Padua: Lice, 1960), 54.
[126] Ciomei, *Il Pugnale*, 60-1.
[127] Ibid., 61-2.
[128] Ibid., 60-1.

35: As a True Son of St. Francis

Alessandro's living arrangements had to be resolved, so he went back to Corinaldo to see the archpriest again. He hosted Alessandro in his rectory for a few days, and they considered a new solution, still oriented towards a religious order. The good parish priest wrote to various communities. Soon, he had a choice. He could go and live with the Passionists in Jesi or with the Capuchins in Ascoli Piceno. Since Alessandro already knew the Capuchins, and, all things considered, what happened in Amandola was not their fault, he chose them.

The Capuchins had been in Ascoli Piceno, the principal city in the lower part of the Marches, since 1569. Their convent is located near the cemetery. Though the church is dedicated to Our Lady, its fame was due to the presence of St. Serafino da Montegranaro (1540–1604), a Capuchin brother. He was known as a holy friar who went through the countryside begging alms. In addition to his role as porter in the convent of Ascoli, he had a lot of contact with people of his era. He always consoled the poor and suffering with a word and his holy presence. He was canonized by Pope Clement XIII in 1767, and his remains are venerated in the Capuchin church in Ascoli.

"My odyssey was then over," Alessandro commented upon arriving in the convent of Ascoli Piceno. Unfortunately, we do not know the exact date of his arrival. The Capuchin archives did not record the arrival of Alessandro Serenelli. In any case, he would live there for almost twenty years.

It is important to clarify Serenelli's choice. Alessandro did not become a friar; that is, he never took vows within the Capuchin Order. He never requested it, nor would it have been possible canonically. Instead, he lived within the Franciscan community while remaining in the lay state. Alessandro was as a guest, beloved and respected, and well-integrated in the dynamics of convent life.

Though he was never a Capuchin, Alessandro lived out the Franciscan ideal in an exemplary manner. "He lived as a true son of St. Francis," to borrow the phrase most frequently used by his contemporary Capuchins in describing his way of life with them. From the day he set foot within the Sanctuary of Ambro in 1937 until his death on May 6, 1970, Alessandro breathed deeply the air of Franciscan spirituality. It was vital for him in serving to improve his relationships with people and with God.

Alessandro described life with the friars in Ascoli.

> I lived in the Capuchin convent in Ascoli for almost twenty years. The convent has a beautiful vegetable garden, which has a lot of water and is completely flat. The church sanctuary encloses the body of St. Serafino, a Capuchin friar, in a bronze urn. [...] The convent, secluded from the world, with its silent corridors, the church, was for me in those long years like an oasis for the thirsty, a refuge for the sailor. I was assigned a simple room in a small corridor. In the convent during those years, I had various assignments. I spent the first few years working in the garden. I got up early in the morning, watered, dug, looked after the trees, and sowed the land. It was a difficult, though varied, life. It was my life. My passion for the land has accompanied me since my childhood. But by 1945, I stopped working as a gardener and was assigned the role of porter, that is, being a doorman. I was tasked with opening the door and trying to please many people—not the simplest thing in the world. Furthermore, the years were starting to weigh on me. Climbing the stairs 100 times a day was a true sacrifice. Even though I was never a friar, in serving as porter, I really began to become a friar, that is, to exercise patience. It is known that, in addition to good people, people from all walks of life arrive at the door. Many are demanding, insatiable, and even curious. [129]

There are many photos of Serenelli during this period. They show him in the garden or opening the door of the convent. He always appears enveloped in a great inner peace, which he certainly communicated to others.

---

[129] Ciomei, *Il Pugnale*, 62-4.

36: A Converted Man

The following was written by a visitor to the Capuchin convent in Ascoli Piceno.

His days in the convent were characterized by most holy monotony. He always got up both in winter and in summer at 3:00 a.m. In the summer, after reciting his prayers, he engaged in various chores until Mass. In winter, when the sun rises later, he stayed in his room and usually meditated with his head in his hands while leaning on the little desk. During the day, his duties as porter kept him occupied in holy busyness, aware that work has expiatory value in the earthly paradise. He prayed often and trusted blindly in his Protectress, while the thought of his crime never left him. To the Father Guardian who complained that it never rained, he exclaimed, "I wish it rained so much water that it were to wash away the blood stains of my life. I still have to atone. If the water of the Tronto River, which passes through Ascoli, had the power to wash the hands of criminals, I would stand day and night with my hands immersed in the stream." Without a doubt, he lived in hope and certainty of Maria's forgiveness. He was sure that she prayed for him, and he was sure that she wanted him close to her in Heaven. The moral certainty of his salvation imbued his entire life with a sweet and serene spirituality. During the day, he read books by ascetics and recited the Holy Rosary. Before lying down at night, he kneeled before a picture of Marietta he kept above his bed. The picture is an important memory because it has this dedication, "Ersilia Goretti, sister of the Blessed [gave this] to

A CONVERTED MAN

Alessandro Serenelli, 1947." He recited the Our Father, which he continuously recited during his imprisonment. Then, looking up to his Protectress, he said, "Marietta, fulfill the promise: take me with you to Heaven." Having uttered these words, Alessandro experienced a profound consolation that helped him sleep. If I were to describe the spiritual figure of Alessandro in two words, I would say that he is a "holy penitent." Upon leaving the convent, we had the impression of having experienced a scene of the ancient penitents of the desert, and the words of St. Paul emerged on our lips, "where sin increased, grace overflowed all the more" (Romans 5:20). [130]

Alessandro was in Ascoli Piceno during the period of Maria Goretti's Beatification. He recalled the period.

Just as water from the large basin flowed out into our garden, the fame of sanctity of the girl I killed also spread. I, too, went to Rome to testify in the various canonical processes on her life and virtue. I heard about the miracles obtained by several people who had resorted to her intercession. Until then, I had recited prayers of suffrage to her, but now I prayed to her to forgive my crime and to be the Protectress of my life, to be for me what the star is for the sailor. I wasn't worthy, but she gave me hope with her forgiveness. In April 1947, her Beatification was celebrated in Rome. I discussed with the [Capuchin] Fathers several times the advisability of me attending the ceremony. Some said that my presence would be a "dark point" of the celebration, while others highlighted that the presence of her converted murderer would be the most beautiful crown for the new Blessed. I was personally against it. I already imagined the frenzy of photographers, journalists, and above all, the curiosity of women, and how I would be pointed at. At a certain point, the superiors decided that I should participate. But God arranged otherwise. The priest responsible for accompanying me to Rome died suddenly just before we were scheduled to leave, and everyone saw this as a sign from Heaven. Instead, I accepted the invitation to attend the celebration in Corinaldo to commemorate the great event. Assunta lived there and welcomed me with open arms, and this reminded me of that great Christmas night in 1934. I arrived in Corinaldo by car from Senigallia. Talking to another passenger, I said that I was coming from Ascoli Piceno. "Maria's killer lives there," said the passenger. "I heard that too," I replied. "Do you happen to know him?" he asked. "Yes, I know him well." "Is it true that he became a Capuchin friar?" "No," I said firmly. "He is not a religious. He's a worker, like me." Once I arrived in Corinaldo, I went to the little house of Assunta, who lived with her daughter Ersilia. Everyone was happy to see me, especially Marietta's nephews and nieces, who met me for the first time. Assunta introduced me to them with these exact words, "This is the gentleman who opened the door to Heaven for Aunt Maria. Thanks to him, she is now blessed." I was amazed by such graciousness. Then she told me privately that she had great joy. "It's natural. Having a blessed daughter is the height of happiness for a mother," I said. "Not only for this," replied Mamma Assunta. "It is because now all my relatives have forgiven you. Maria can now be happy with all of us." As she said this, her eyes shone with joy. The celebration was grand but also filled with spirituality, and this calmed my soul. Then I returned to my "refuge" in Ascoli even more determined to continue the life of penance and solitude I had imposed on myself. [131]

Between Maria's beatification and canonization, an event took place that increased the worldwide fame of St. Maria Goretti. Augusto Genina, a well-known director of Italian neorealism, released his film on Marietta's life with the legendary title *Cielo Sulla Palude* (*Heaven over the Marshes*). The figure of the saint emerges in a context of great poverty and misery, where faith represents the only driving force of her values and hopes. The scenery of the Pontine Marshes was admirable, and young Ines Orsini's interpretation of Maria was convincing.

The role of Alessandro was not easy. Genina probably did not delve deeply into the writing of Serenelli's character. Alessandro was told about the film by the Capuchin fathers, but his opinion about it was not enthusiastic.

> In 1949, *Heaven over the Marshes* was released. It was well received and even won the Prime Minister's Award. I don't judge the film from an artistic point of view, as I'm not competent to do so. But, as recommended by the Capuchin Fathers, I never went to see it. Yet I know that there were exaggerations, inconsistencies, falsehoods, and even injustices. We shall not talk about me, whom they harassed in 1,000 ways, or about the sea that Maria saw alone, or if she saw it, from the train window. Then, my father was depicted in a very bad light. Poor dad! He didn't deserve it. They made him appear violent, not at all affectionate, and addicted to wine and vices. Instead, I recall him as being good to his family, an excellent worker, and full of good will and sacrifice. Sure, he wasn't interested in new ideas. Though I was a boy at the time, I never saw him behave badly. After the film, several lawyers suggested that I file a lawsuit for defamation and compensation for moral damages. Instead, I told them that it doesn't matter, that [I accept it] all as expiation for my crime. Like the film, the press was not evenhanded or objective towards me, and they spread false and unfounded news. [132]

No one considered what Alessandro experienced throughout all this. The media looked for the sensational and flashy. But nothing was revealed of the inner life of Alessandro. Instead, the "murderer of the Saint" chose a secondary role—silence. It wasn't easy for him to carry the weight of such an uncomfortable and unprecedented role.

---

[130] Informative Process, 166-7.
[131] Ciomei, *Il Pugnale*, 64.
[132] Pujadas, *Yo maté*, 163-4.

37: Farewell to Mamma Assunta

When Alessandro's father partnered with the Gorettis in Colle Gianturco (Paliano) at the end of 1898, he did so in large part because he and his son did not have a family. Assunta—then thirty-two years old—was married with four children; later, two more would be born. Despite the fact that they were separated by only sixteen years of age, surely this shady, taciturn, and arrogant boy—that is, Alessandro—discovered in Assunta a maternal role model. He would have observed the love with which she looked after her children. As someone who never had a mother, he would likely have projected onto her his many dreams and expectations.

Assunta, on the other hand, after learning of Alessandro's sad childhood and the plight of his mother, Cecilia, surely sought to extend to him her good will, notwithstanding Giovanni Serenelli's questionable character. Her description of Alessandro—that is, before July 5, 1902—was overall positive. "He was a physically well-developed and robust young man, assiduous at work, respectful toward his father and towards me. He was a bit withdrawn. And when he wasn't working, he closed himself in his room, absorbed in his reading." [133]

There are references from some of the early biographies that highlight Assunta's maternal role towards Alessandro. Once, she reprimanded Alessandro for the photos he had attached to the wall of the room. Though he responded brusquely, "If you don't like them, don't look at them," her reproach was also aimed at him. She intended to protect "all" of her children from certain influences in order to form them according to a certain upbringing, which unfortunately Alessandro had not had.

Another time, when Alessandro was feeling frustrated over his future, he was grumpier and more resentful towards Marietta than usual. Assunta told her daughter, "Be patient. He will soon enter the military." [134] Even though she was seeking to encourage her daughter, she was also considering what might be fulfilling to Alessandro.

As for the rest, the extended family dynamic—typical in that era—was apparently normal. However, when darkness fell over the Cascina Antica and Marietta revealed to her mother what had taken place before the horrendous attack, Assunta felt betrayed. It was as if she had been violated by her godson.

Assunta's reproaches should be understood to this end. If news of his "temptations" had reached Maria's mother's ears, with the authority she exercised over Alessandro Serenelli, surely, events would have taken a different turn. In fact, Alessandro feared Assunta, her authority, her prestige, and her strong temperament.

After the attack, the interfamily dynamic ended, and everyone went their own way. Meanwhile, Maria Goretti's "star" rose. Above all, her act of forgiveness spread; it even became catechetical. Assunta was the first disciple of Marietta, the child of God. Her maternal instinct for Alessandro was now elevated to a different level. Sewing a button or hemming a shirt was no longer the issue. Instead, her concern was that of the eternal salvation of the murderer of her daughter. Assunta did her part so that Marietta's wish—"I want him near me in Heaven"—would be realized.

The first fruits were revealed at the end of the criminal trial in Rome. On the afternoon of October 15, 1902, Assunta's voice was loud and clear. When she announced that she forgave Alessandro, word spread beyond the courtroom, causing a stir throughout Rome. It was not an isolated episode, a mere moment of emotional exuberance. Later, after he was imprisoned, Assunta sought to contact Alessandro. Decades later, when he was released from prison and came to Corinaldo on Christmas 1934, Assunta embraced him yet again in an act of forgiveness that moved the hearts of the people.

Alessandro's subsequent return trips to Corinaldo were always marked by a climate of reconciliation and affection on the part of the entire Goretti family, even if there were different nuances. Photographs from the 1940s and 1950s reveal two elderly people—Assunta and Alessandro—talking to one another with serenity that only God can convey.

Assunta experienced firsthand the great celebrations of her daughter's beatification and canonization. By then, Assunta had assumed global notoriety. In 1952, on the fiftieth anniversary of Maria's martyrdom, Pope Pius XII wrote Assunta a personal letter. In that era, popes virtually never addressed ordinary people.

Alessandro saw Assunta the last time in September 1954. He recounted that final encounter in a moving way. "We were photographed together, and I told her, 'Assunta, we have grown old,' to which she responded, 'Let us thank God that we have come this far.'" [135]

Toward the beginning of October, Ersilia sent a telegram to Serenelli, saying that Assunta had only a few days left. Alessandro described what happened next.

> I left immediately. I had to be there. It was the last meeting, the last testimony of my gratitude and affection. I arrived in Corinaldo in the evening and anxiously climbed the stairs. But she was already deceased. I kneeled down, kissed her hand tenderly, and prayed heartily for her. A solemn funeral was celebrated. She was accompanied by many people, including priests, religious, and associations. [136]

Assunta Goretti died on October 8, 1954. Alessandro's memoirs conclude with a beautiful portrait of the maternal woman who, more than anyone else, understood and defended him.

> I have many good memories of her in my mind for having spent those years together. And then, above all, her forgiveness and the embrace she extended to me that Christmas evening in Corinaldo! They told me that after the President of the Court read the sentence, he turned to her and asked her if she forgave me. She replied yes. Then there was murmuring in the courtroom saying, "I wouldn't forgive him." But she said, "What if God didn't forgive us?" To me, she is truly a holy woman. If I had to talk about her, I would need an entire book. [137]

Assunta Carlini is buried in Corinaldo in the diocesan sanctuary of St. Maria Goretti. Her remains are interred on the left side of the nave. On the tombstone are simply the words, MAMMA ASSUNTA. Yes, she was a mother to Maria and her natural children. But she was also a mother to Alessandro—the murderer of her daughter.

Some years after his death, Alessandro's body were moved from the cemetery of Macerata, where he was initially buried, to Corinaldo. His remains are now interred on the right side of the nave of the sanctuary now dedicated to St. Maria Goretti. Today, the mother and murderer of Maria Goretti rest together. The story of Assunta and Alessandro is not only a moving example of Christian forgiveness and reconciliation; it reveals the purity of the Gospel: that love "bears all things, believes all things, hopes all things, endures all things" (1 Corinthians 13:7).

---

[133] Stella. *Il martirio*, 55.
[134] Ciomei, *Il Pugnale*, 68.
[135] Ibid.
[136] Ibid.
[137] Audience Capuchin Convent, Macerata, 172-83.

38: The Testament

The Capuchin convent in Macerata is located up on a hill just beyond the railway. The red brick structure and church are shaded due to a lovely canopy of trees surrounding the complex. On the right side of the church is the wooden door leading into the convent. This door was opened and closed by Alessandro Serenelli, in his role as porter. After a small sitting room, there is a corridor. Beyond the window in the rear, one can see the large vegetable garden, where Alessandro worked. Along one of the rear corridors, on the right, is cell number twenty. It is currently occupied by an infirmed Capuchin friar. There is no sign or anything exceptional about it. Yet this was Alessandro's cell for fourteen years. Everywhere, there are handrails, as well as elderly friars in wheelchairs. Since the cells are on the ground floor, rendering stairs unnecessary for the elderly friars, the Macerata convent has always served as the infirmary for the Capuchin friars of the Province of the Marches.

After living with the Capuchins in Ascoli Piceno for eighteen years, Alessandro requested to be transferred to Macerata. By 1956, his strength was failing and he was advancing in age. The Capuchins did not send him away. Instead, with fine human and Christian sensitivity, they accepted his request. He arrived in Macerata on November 17, 1956. For the next fourteen years, after Assunta's death, he was one of the last personal witnesses to St. Maria Goretti and the horrible "deed."

Alessandro had now fully embraced the secluded life in the Capuchin convent. He had atoned for his sins and was grateful for all that had happened. Above all, he never asked anyone for favors. This is how he concludes his memoirs.

> Close to the end of my days, I have only to pray and live in anticipation [of Heaven]. I pray for myself and for many who write to me asking for prayers. Letters arrive from all over Italy, France, Germany, Switzerland, and even America. In the evening, in my little cell, before the small painting of St. Maria Goretti, I pray, light candles, and say the Rosary. God's mercy is truly infinite. I pray, waiting for the promise made to me by the saint on her deathbed to be fulfilled. [138]

In this scenario of solitude and conscientious waiting, on May 5, 1961, Alessandro Serenelli wrote his spiritual testament. It was his highest moment. Here it is in its entirety.

> I am almost eighty years old, near to closing my day. Looking back at my past, I recognize that in my early youth I followed a false road: the way of evil that led to ruin. Through the press, I saw the shows and bad examples that the majority of young people are following that path without reflecting on it, and I, too, did not concern myself with it. Around me, I had practicing believers, but I took no notice, blinded by a brute force that pushed me down the bad road. At the age of twenty, I committed a crime of passion, of which today I am horrified by the memory alone. Maria Goretti, now a Saint, was the good angel whom Providence placed before my steps to save me. I still have impressed in my heart her words of rebuke and forgiveness. She prayed for me; she interceded for her killer. Thirty years of imprisonment followed. If I had not been a minor, I would have been sentenced to life. I accepted the sentence I deserved; resigned, I expiated my sin. Maria was truly my light, my Protectress; with her help, I behaved well in the twenty-seven years in prison and tried to live honestly when society accepted me back among its members. The Sons of St. Francis, the Capuchin Minors of the Marches, with seraphic charity, welcomed me among them not as a servant but as a brother. With them, I have lived since 1936. And now I await serenely the moment to be admitted to the vision of God, to embrace once again my loved ones, and to be close to my Angel Protectress

and her dear mother, Assunta. May those who read this letter of mine desire to draw on the happy teaching of avoiding evil and always following good from childhood. May they believe that Religion with its precepts is not something they can do without but is the true comfort, the only sure way in all circumstances, even the most painful ones of life.

Peace and all good. Alessandro Serenelli. [139]

Alessandro's Testament is a compendium of a long life regenerated by the pedagogy of forgiveness. It proposes to new generations a way of life while expressing gratitude to the Capuchin friars for having received him. We see the reflection of the image of "the head of a household who brings from his storeroom both the new and the old" (Matthew 13:52)—all for the building up of that "Kingdom" that will come, but which already flourishes within us in this world here and now. Alessandro reached for that Kingdom with all his strength.

---

[138] Ciomei, *Il Pugnale*, 69.
[139] Ibid., 65-6.

39: May 6, 1970

Alessandro corresponded with many people from all over Italy: Capuchin friars, relatives, ex-prisoners, and chaplains. We have read many letters that he sent to members of the Goretti family. His handwriting is rounded and simple. It is a polite but direct way of asking the question, and it encompasses a sense of humility and peace.

Now, we shall allow the Capuchin storytelling tradition to speak of Alessandro. There are many interesting stories and anecdotes handed down among the Capuchins themselves, which have been made known to the public. Naturally, every friar who lived with him during those years had something to say about him, almost like relics shared with those who, through St. Maria Goretti, approached his stormy human adventure.

Fra Urbano, whose task was to tend to the friars in the infirmary convent of Macerata, recalls the following.

> How many times in these years have the people who have come to visit him told him, "Blessed are you who will go to Heaven, because Maria Goretti promised it to you," to which he replied, "It is not true, it's not true; one has to deserve Heaven." [140] But I believe that he really deserved it. He followed our Franciscan rule of life with the utmost scrupulosity, with a Christian spirit that only a man who has achieved true peace of soul can have. His work as porter alternated with those of correspondence with the numerous devotees of the saint who flocked to the good Alessandro to intercede to Marietta. A telegram arrived for Alessandro which said, "I ask for your blessing and your prayers to save my family from a desperate case." Signed, a

devotee of St. Maria Goretti. Included was a signature and address with paid return postage. I read it aloud in a moving tone, but Alessandro could no longer hear well. He looked on without understanding. He raised his hand with a wave and said, "If everyone has forgiven me, I will pass away serenely." [141]

Forgiveness was the constant theme of his existence. It was the reason for his inner peace, the breath of his soul, and the drive to never give up. He was a living demonstration that forgiveness heals and regenerates. In him, the words of Jesus gave new life, an earthquake with unexpected consequences.

Some year before Alessandro's death, he wanted to create something concrete regarding this notion. With the little savings he had, he commissioned a wooden sculpture to be erected in the Capuchin church of Ancona, depicting "Marietta's forgiveness of Alessandro." The artist was the renowned Giuseppe Stuflesser from Ortisei from the Dolomite Mountains.

On February 15, 1970, while going down the steps of the church, Alessandro slipped and fell badly, fracturing his right femur. He was taken to the hospital. Given his age, eighty-eight, they could not operate. He was taken back to the convent. From that moment on, he remained bedridden. Sunset was near for Alessandro. Several times he declared openly, "I am ready to go to Heaven to reach St. Maria Goretti, who awaits me." [142]

The end came suddenly. On Wednesday, May 6, 1970, the eve of the Ascension, he died. Precisely seventy years earlier, Luigi Goretti, the father of the future saint, died in the Pontine Marshes, struck down by malaria. But let's leave it to the friars who were I the convent to tell the story of the final days and moments of Alessandro Serenelli. The following was chronicled by Fr. Gilberto da Sarnano.

> At 7:00 p.m., assisted by Fr. Gilberto, in the presence of Fr. Donato da Loro Piceno and Br. Vito da Montegiorgio, Alessandro Serenelli—the man who murdered St. Maria Goretti, the martyr of purity, in the now distant July 5, 1902, in the locality of Le Ferriere di Nettuno (Rome)—passed away peacefully. Serenelli had been a guest of our infirmary since November 17, 1956. A guest helper in our

convent in Ascoli, he was transferred to the infirmary by the Most Reverend Father Gabriele da Colli del Tronto, Provincial Vicar of that time, since the Provincial Father Alfredo da Ostra was on a Sacred Visit to the Custody of Bahia (Brazil). [We] religious were under no civil duty to take care of the elderly and infirmed Serenelli, but given his international fame for the canonization of his victim, it was deemed appropriate to host him in this infirmary rather than admitting him to a hospice for the elderly, as Serenelli himself and Fr. Andrea da Potenza Picena, Superior of Ascoli, who received him as a helper in 1936, had both accorded. During the years of his stay in this infirmary, Serenelli was noted for having a spirit of prayer on par with, if not superior to, that of a good religious friar. He was always present in the chapel for all the practices of piety common to religious, including daily Eucharistic Communion. Even outside of the [liturgical] hours, he was often in the chapel praying. He spent his day in his cell reading books and magazines he borrowed from the common reading room. He was an avid reader. Due to poor blood circulation, he suffered much in his legs, but he never complained about his ailments, and, when he could, he sought to be useful to the other residents. In his final illness, which confined him to bed for almost three months, he was always serene and resigned with a great spirit of endurance. During the dressing of bedsores, which at times must have been very painful, the only expression that came out of his lips was, "Our Lady, how it hurts!"; otherwise, he called the names of those who treated him. There was never an expression of impatience; on the contrary, often a thank you of gratitude. Once the dressing was complete, he remained immobile, in the supine position, for hours and hours, without a complaint, without ever calling or ringing the bell for relief. When he had visits, he liked to end them with a nod to Heaven and with the promise to "pray for everyone." On the occasion of Serenelli's final illness and death, many articles were written, and many inaccurate things were said. The press, in general, wanted to make him out to be a great penitent and a saint. He certainly wasn't a great penitent, if by penitent we mean someone who embraced deprivations and physical sufferings, like self-flogging, wearing hairshirts, etc. Was he a saint? At least outwardly, he gave no sign of it. In the opinion of this chronicler, Alessandro Serenelli was a man who had repented of his sin and faced his years of prison and those afterwards with a serenity of spirit that befits those who are aware of having been forgiven by the mercy of God and his victim, and at the same time was reassured by the certainty of having an assured Protectress in Heaven in the one who was martyred in the throes of impure passion. Pope Pius XII, on the occasion of the Beatification of Maria Goretti, rightly referred to Serenelli as a "repentant and rehabilitated man." These two words summarize Serenelli's life after that tragic day of July 5, 1902. In the final moments of his life, I, Father Gilberto, who was next to him reciting the prayers of the dying, noticed that Alessandro kept his eyes fixed, though not wide open, on a point on the opposite wall. Perhaps that which a columnist wrote in his final paragraph had occurred, "Alessandro certainly listened in the last moments." A second before expiring, he closed his eyes and his mouth and assumed a very serene mien. So he remained until the closing of the coffin, which took place on the afternoon of May 8 in the mortuary of the [municipal] cemetery. Throughout the entirety of the day on May 7, Serenelli's body lay in repose in the room for the deceased, cell no. 20, on the ground floor of the infirmary. As it was a public holiday, the Ascension, an orderly influx of visitors, divided into small groups of five to six people, entered one after another for almost the entire day. Three young great-nephews of Alessandro witnessed this demonstration of affection from the people of Macerata towards their great-uncle. The funeral took place on the eighth. At 9:30 a.m., there was Holy Mass concelebrated by the Father Superior, assisted by two lay friars. Then Alessandro was transported to the city cemetery. There was no large flux of people, as some mistakenly believed. Present were the bishop of Macerata, who gave a special eulogy; some diocesan priests; and [Capuchin] friars from Recanati, San Severino Marche, and Ascoli Piceno, where Serenelli, as has been remembered, worked for twenty years as a helper. His body was buried in the cemetery of Macerata in niche no. 15109, which Serenelli himself had purchased a few years earlier. The niche is sealed with a marble plaque with a photograph of the deceased and the writing, "ALESSANDRO SERENELLI, born on June 2, 1882, died on May 6, 1970. [143]

After his funeral, in the desk drawer [in his cell], the Capuchins found a yellowed envelope. Inside it, written in ink, was his spiritual Testament. Along with it, there was a rolled-up note that said, "I ask forgiveness from the world for the outrage I did to the martyr Maria Goretti and to [her] purity. I urge young people to stay away from immoral shows, dangers, and occasions that can lead to sin."

This final sentence encapsulates Alessandro Serenelli's human and Christian journey, in which the darkness of the past has been transformed into a ray of light for future generations. May he be an example to all, especially to those who have committed serious sins. May they, too, come to awareness of the profound mercy of God.

---

[140] Ciomei, *Il Pugnale*, 71.
[141] Audience Capuchin Convent, 172-83.
[142] Ciomei, *Il Pugnale*, 73.
[143] Ibid., 28.

Appendix

The Prodigal Son
(Luke 15:11-32)

A man had two sons, and the younger son said to his father, "Father, give me the share of your estate that should come to me." So the father divided the property between them.

After a few days, the younger son collected all his belongings and set off to a distant country where he squandered his inheritance on a life of dissipation.

When he had freely spent everything, a severe famine struck that country, and he found himself in dire need.

So he hired himself out to one of the local citizens who sent him to his farm to tend the swine.

And he longed to eat his fill of the pods on which the swine fed, but nobody gave him any.

Coming to his senses he thought, "How many of my father's hired workers have more than enough food to eat, but here am I, dying from hunger. I shall get up and go to my father and I shall say to him, 'Father, I have sinned against heaven and against you. I no longer deserve to be called your son; treat me as you would treat one of your hired workers.'"

So he got up and went back to his father. While he was still a long way off, his father caught sight of him, and was filled with compassion. He ran to his son, embraced him and kissed him.

His son said to him, "Father, I have sinned against heaven and against you; I no longer deserve to be called your son."

But his father ordered his servants, "Quickly bring the finest robe and put it on him; put a ring on his finger and sandals on his feet. Take the fattened calf and slaughter it. Then let us celebrate with a feast, because this son of mine was dead, and has come to life again; he was lost, and has been found." Then the celebration began.

Now the older son had been out in the field and, on his way back, as he neared the house, he heard the sound of music and dancing. He called one of the servants and asked what this might mean.

The servant said to him, "Your brother has returned and your father has slaughtered the fattened calf because he has him back safe and sound."

He became angry, and when he refused to enter the house, his father came out and pleaded with him.

He said to his father in reply, "Look, all these years I served you and not once did I disobey your orders; yet you never gave me even a young goat to feast on with my friends. But when your son returns who swallowed up your property with prostitutes, for him you slaughter the fattened calf."

He said to him, "My son, you are here with me always; everything I have is yours. But now we must celebrate and rejoice, because your brother was dead and has come to life again; he was lost and has been found."

The Cross and Forgiveness
Father Jean Galot, S.J.

The torture of the cross reveals Jesus' willingness to take on the weight of humanity's sins. He obtains for all full liberation from this burden. On the cross itself, he showed us the connection between the cross and forgiveness. He addressed a prayer to the Father, which expressed the intention of the sacrifice and guaranteed its efficaciousness: "Father, forgive them, they know not what they do" (Luke 23:34).

His plea for forgiveness is made particularly for those responsible for the torture of the cross—for those who contributed to the condemnation or participated in the plot that eventually received Pilate's assent. However, beyond those who bear immediate responsibility for the event, the imploring of forgiveness is made for the benefit of all humanity, who receives the fruit of his redemptive offering. Christ's generosity is above all notable for the fact that the Crucifix asks for forgiveness for those who put him on the cross.

According to the Gospel of Luke, these are the first words spoken on the cross. Thus, it appears that not even for an instant did Jesus let feelings of revenge or anger towards those who had sent him to execution enter his heart. He expressly showed that he wanted for them the fullness of forgiveness.

He not only asks for the Father's forgiveness but justifies this supplication by excusing those who unleashed themselves against him and showed him their hostility. He dares to say to defend them: "They know not what they do," because it is the truth, a truth that he knows perfectly, with a gaze that reaches the depths of the human conscience. Apparently the adversaries knew what they were doing: Caiaphas had advised putting Jesus to death so that the entire nation would not be ruined (see John 11:50). Pilate, after having declared several times that Jesus was innocent, sentenced him to the torture of the cross. Despite this external evidence of personal responsibility of the Jewish high priest and the Roman governor, Jesus' statement invites us to admit that their responsibility was attenuated, to the point that one can find a serious reason for the forgiveness implored. Jesus became the advocate of his enemies by affirming their ignorance of the true extent of the condemnation.

The interpretation given by Christ makes us reflect on responsibility in crimes and in personal fault: guilt can be much less extensive than what is suggested by appearance. We do not know the depth of the conscience.

Objectively, the condemnation of Jesus is the most serious crime in the history of humanity. But subjectively, we do not know the degree of responsibility of those who played a role in it. We must also recognize that all people share a certain responsibility, for the fact that all are sinners and that the crucifixion of Jesus was due to the sin of the world.

The plea for forgiveness is addressed to the Father. Since it comes from the Son, who has perfectly fulfilled the Father's will by offering his sacrifice of the cross, the supplication was completely successful. The Father responded positively to the Son's prayer.

This is how the victory of Christ appears before being confirmed by the resurrection. It is the victory of love that brings with it forgiveness. The words pronounced by Jesus at the moment he was lifted up on the cross signify the intimate personal victory over all the claims of revenge and hatred in the world. The Savior's only response to his adversaries is that of the most generous love that asks for forgiveness and obtains it with the heroic gift of himself.

The plea for forgiveness imprints a smile on the cross that announces the new humanity promised to the deepest peace, that of the forgiven soul.

Stages of Forgiveness

All humanity is called to love. But how can we love when we are hurt by those around us, perhaps by those whom we love most? Expectations of their love are unfulfilled due to difficulties of daily life—signs of affection we do not receive, harmful words, and so on. But by grace, forgiveness can restore harmony.

But then the harm comes back to mind, and the heart is overwhelmed again by rancor, resentment, and even hatred. Yet had there not been forgiveness? Had words of forgiveness not been spoken? Was this not enough? What else is needed?

Below are suggested stages to follow in order to fully embrace forgiveness.

BECOME AWARE OF THE HURT

Forgiving is not forgetting; it would not be possible to forgive if one no longer recalled the hurt. We must learn to look at our hurts in order to determine their origins. Why does someone who has been betrayed suffer? Is it because of their affections or because they were disappointed in their expectations? This step is possible in prayer. The Holy Spirit will highlight the sin present in these types of sufferings: for example, if pride has been wounded, which is not the same thing as a pierced, disinterested love.

Here there is the risk of falling into two traps: minimizing the hurt or rejecting the one who committed the offense by identifying that person with their fault. The best attitude is to recognize, through who I am, the reasons for my suffering. Perhaps I had idealized my husband or child, and I was disappointed; perhaps that ideal is destroyed. Or, maybe the hurt touched an old wound in me—one not yet healed. This could be a sense of guilt or a sense of inferiority.

CONSIDER THE OFFENDER IN A POSITIVE LIGHT

The first response to being hurt is usually perceiving the person who has committed an offense negatively: they become the evil act they committed. Instead, to cast a positive gaze on that person is to recognize that they are capable of other things. If we cannot accept good things about this person, it is a sign that forgiveness has not been granted. In prayer, we need to return to the previous stage to discover how this person has hurt us but also to discover that they are lovable. We ask for the grace to see them as God sees them.

PRONOUNCE WORDS OF BLESSING

Those who cause suffering are sent by God so that love can grow. Learning to forgive means becoming vulnerable and loving those who hurt us. This is drawn from the Gospel: "But I say to you, love your enemies, and pray for those who persecute you" (Matthew 5:44). Life in community and family begins here: love those who do harm. Let the Holy Spirit act; he will give the words of blessing, words that foster love. To do so, we use the correct weapons: prayer, meditation on the Word of God, and the sacraments.

CARRY OUT CONCRETE ACTS

An important stage is to demonstrate our forgiveness with concrete gestures. Show the person who committed the offense that we truly love them through charitable acts. But this stage must not be anticipated. It is first necessary for a period of time to pass from the initial emotional reaction. Forgiveness requires a process; it is not an event. Good acts come only after one has fully healed from the harm that was committed.

ONLY GOD CAN CONQUER EVIL

Only God can forgive sins and forgive the sinner that we are. Yet Jesus tells us in Scripture, handed down to us in the Our Father, to ask the Father to "forgive us our debts, as we forgive our debtors" (Matthew 6:12). Does God place a condition on our forgiveness? Yes, because the life we received at baptism is at stake. To forgive is to experience rebirth into a new life. Refusing forgiveness is to reject that love, to reject that new life.

FRUITS OF FORGIVENESS

The fruits of forgiveness are many, and they are beautiful. Here, we will consider two: openness and tenderness of heart.

If dialogue is no longer possible, it is often because we have not fully forgiven. In this case, openness is often a cause for condemnation. Instead, we need to know how to be patient and to have fully passed through the stages of forgiveness in order to be in the light. Then, openness will be a blessing. Each person can reveal themselves to the other as they are, in all their simplicity. Communion is then appreciated, something has been freed, and love can grow.

Once forgiveness has taken place, one can remain in suffering for a very long time. Do not be surprised. On the contrary, it is good to welcome this suffering, offer it, and leave it with all its power to transform us. It is the door that opens to tenderness of the heart. A single wound to the heart can render our affections supernatural. This protects us from rebelling, which is not true compassion.

We may never have the tenderness that we offer to others. Instead, we can be filled with it the day we begin to see the fruit of forgiveness, which is a supernatural tenderness. At that point, we will be inhabited by the tenderness of the Father, the divine presence, and which we give to others. This is a free love that fills us up and that we can give to and fill others.

Prayers of Forgiveness
Father Robert DeGrandis, SSJ

Lord Jesus, I turn to You today and ask for the grace to forgive anyone who has ever offended me throughout my entire life. I know that You will give me the fortitude to forgive. I thank You because You love me more than I love myself, and You want my happiness more than I can desire it.

Lord Jesus, I want to be free from resentments and the anguish and inflexibility I had towards You. I ask Your forgiveness for all the times I believed that it was You who sent death, suffering, economic difficulties, punishments, or illnesses into my family. Lord, purify my mind and heart today.

Lord, I now want to forgive myself for my own sins, shortcomings, and failures. I want to forgive myself for all that is wrong or evil inside me or for that which I believe is evil.

I forgive myself for any participation in occultism, such as in tarot cards. I forgive myself for having believed in horoscopes, for having consulted fortune tellers or seers, or for having possessed or worn amulets. I renounce all these superstitions and choose You alone as my Lord and Savior. Fill me with Your Holy Spirit.

I forgive myself for having spoken Your Name in vain or for having blasphemed, for not having worshipped You, for not having honored You as I should have, and for having failed to participate in the Holy Mass.

I forgive myself for any opposition against my parents; for becoming intoxicated or taking drugs; and for all sins against purity, such as fornication, adultery, or abortion. I forgive myself for stealing and for any lies I have ever told. I sincerely repent and forgive myself for all of these things and for any other wrongs I am guilty of.
  THANK YOU, LORD, FOR THE GRACE YOU GIVE ME.

I sincerely forgive my MOTHER. I forgive her for all times she offended me, when she showed resentment towards me, or when she got angry with me and punished me. I forgive her for the times she preferred my siblings over me. I forgive her for all the offensive words she said to me, such as calling me stupid, idiot, or bad; for the times she called me the worst of her children; for telling me that I cost the family money; for telling me that I wasn't wanted, that I was born by mistake, that I wasn't the child she wanted; and for focusing on the negative parts of me.
    LORD, TODAY, I FORGIVE HER.

I forgive my FATHER for the times he didn't help me with my needs or for his lack of love, affection, or attention towards me. I forgive him for not having time for me when I needed or wanted it. I forgive him for any times he may have become intoxicated. I forgive him for arguing and fighting with my mother or siblings. I forgive him for the severity of his punishments, for having abandoned us, for having left home, for having divorced my mother, or for having committed adultery.
    LORD, TODAY, I FORGIVE HIM.

Lord, I wish to extend my forgiveness to my BROTHERS and SISTERS. I forgive those siblings who rejected me, lied about me, hated me, held a grudge against me, or were rivals in competing for the love of our parents. I forgive my siblings who harmed me physically or spiritually, were particularly severe with me by punishing me or making my life difficult, and for any other wrongs they may have done.
    LORD, TODAY, I FORGIVE THEM.

Lord, I forgive my SPOUSE for his/her lack of love, affection, support, consideration, attention, tenderness, or understanding. I forgive him/her for his/her shortcomings, mistakes, defects, and for any words or actions that have hurt me or offended me.
    LORD, TODAY, I FORGIVE HIM/HER.

Jesus, I forgive my CHILDREN for their lack of respect,

obedience, love, attention, help, or understanding. I forgive them for saying false things about me or my spouse, for their bad habits, for abandoning religion and/or the faith, or for any other action or word of theirs that have made me suffer.

>LORD, TODAY, I FORGIVE THEM.

Lord, help me to forgive all other FAMILY MEMBERS: grandparents, uncles, cousins, or nephews, who in some way have interfered in our family. I forgive them for being possessive, imposing their will, causing confusion, causing discord among family members, or inciting one against the other.

>LORD, TODAY, I FORGIVE THEM.

God, I forgive all my IN-LAWS: my father-in-law, mother-in-law, sons-in-law, daughters-in-law, brothers-in-law, or anyone else from my spouse's family who has ever treated me or my family badly or without love. I forgive them for their criticisms, thoughts, actions, or omissions that have caused me or my family harm or made us suffer.

>LORD, TODAY, I FORGIVE THEM.

Jesus, help me to forgive my CO-WORKERS who make my life difficult or otherwise cause hardships for me. I forgive those who burden me with work that should be done by others. I forgive them for gossip, their refusal to collaborate, or their attempts to oust me from my job.

>LORD, TODAY, I FORGIVE THEM.

I forgive my NEIGHBORS: for any noise they make or irritation they cause, the carelessness towards common property, their annoying pets, not putting trash in the appropriate bins, their prejudices, creating discord in the neighborhood, not speaking to me, arguing, or holding grudges against me.

>LORD, TODAY, I FORGIVE THEM.

I forgive my PARISH PRIEST for his lack of support, his unclear explanations, boring sermons, being unfriendly, his lack of friendship, or not having encouraged me as he should have. I forgive the leaders of my parish for not trusting me, esteeming me, or entrusting me with tasks I am suitable to carrying out. I forgive them for any other wrongs done to me or my family members, whether current or past.

LORD, TODAY, I FORGIVE THEM.

Lord, I forgive all those who have DIFFERENT VALUES from me. I forgive those who have accused me, ridiculed me, discriminated against me, made fun of me, or harmed me economically. I forgive those who have a DIFFERENT FAITH and who have attacked me, argued with me in trying to impose their beliefs on me, or attempted to distance my family from the faith.

LORD, TODAY, I FORGIVE THEM.

Lord, I forgive all PROFESSIONALS who have ever harmed me in any way: doctors, nurses, lawyers, judges, politicians, policemen, firefighters, or public transport drivers. I forgive all people whom I have ever hired and who overcharged, did a poor job, or otherwise cheated me.

LORD, TODAY, I FORGIVE THEM.

I forgive my EMPLOYER, for not paying me adequately, not appreciating my work, or for not being kind or reasonable with me. I forgive him/her for becoming angry or hostile with me, passing me over for a promotion I deserved, or never praising me when warranted.

LORD, TODAY, I FORGIVE HIM/HER.

Lord, I forgive my TEACHERS. I forgive those who have ever chastised me, insulted me, or humiliated me; who treated me unfairly or made fun of me; and who called me incapable, stupid, or any other derogatory term. I forgive all those who ever punished me unfairly, held me back, or humiliated me in front of my peers.

Lord, I forgive all FRIENDS who have ever spoken badly of me or did not defend me in such situations. I forgive all those who did not support me, were not available when I needed their help, broke

off all contact with me, or did not pay me back any money I lent them.
>   LORD, TODAY, I FORGIVE THEM.

Lord Jesus, I implore You today to grant me the grace to forgive THE PERSON WHO HAS HURT ME THE MOST IN MY LIFE. Grant me, Lord, the ability to forgive my worst enemy, the one whom I said I would never forgive, and the one who costs me the most to forgive.
>   LORD, TODAY, I FORGIVE HIM/HER.

Thank You, Jesus, for freeing me from the evil that comes from having an unforgiving heart. Holy Spirit, fill me with Your light so that all areas of my mind that are still immersed in darkness shall be illuminated.
>   AMEN. ALLELUIA!

Books by Icona Press

Books in this Series:

St. Maria Goretti: A Journey into Forgiveness and Redemption, by Bret Thoman. Icona Press, 2021.

Following Maria Goretti: A Personal Journey from Her Birthplace to Martyrdom, by Bret Thoman. Icona Press, 2024

Other Books:

The Life of Padre Pio: Mystery, Miracles, and Mission. Icona Press, 2024.

Following Padre Pio: A Journey of Discovery from Pietrelcina to San Giovanni Rotondo. Icona Press, 2024. Second Edition.

Saint Francis of Assisi: Passion, Poverty and the Man Who Transformed the Church. TAN Books, 2016.

Saint Clare of Assisi: Light From the Cloister. TAN Books, 2017.

The Diary of Lucia Fiorentino: Mystic, Visionary, and Early Spiritual Daughter of Padre Pio. Icona Press, 2024.

The Diary of St. Veronica Giuliani: A Compendium: "Tell Everyone Love has been found!" Icona Press, 2023.

The Complete Pilgrim Guide to Italy: Land of Saints and Sanctuaries, Miracles and Mystics. Icona Press, 2024.

A Knight and a Lady: A Journey into the Spirituality of Saints Francis and Clare. Icona Press, 2020.

The Pandemic of Padre Pio: Disciple of Our Lady of Sorrows. Stefano Campanella, translated by Bret Thoman. Icona Press, 2021.

"My Rosary": The Beloved Prayer of an Exorcist. Fr. Gabriele Amorth, translated by Bret Thoman. Icona Press, 2023.

From Worldly Princess to the Foot of the Cross: The Life and Writings of Saint Camilla Battista Varano. Icona Press, 2021.

About the Author

Born and raised in Atlanta, Georgia (USA), Bret Thoman, OFS lives in Loreto, Italy with his wife and three children. He has been a member of the Secular Franciscan Order (Third Order of St. Francis) since 2003. He has a master's degree in Italian from Middlebury College, a BA from the University of Georgia in foreign languages, and a certificate in Franciscan Studies.

While working as an interpreter for CNN, Bret translated the papal conclave and announced the election of Pope Francis live. He is also a former commercial pilot and has logged over 3,500 hours of flight time.

Bret's main activity is organizing pilgrimages for St. Francis Pilgrimages, the company he started in 2004. He leads pilgrims throughout Italy, the Holy Land, and along the walking Caminos in Italy.

In his leisure time, Bret enjoys reading, hiking, sailing his Laser sailboat in the Adriatic Sea, and visiting new places.

All Bret's books are online at:
www.amazon.com/Bret-Thoman/e/B0753K2PTJ

He can be contacted at bret@stfrancispilgrimages.com

Did this book help you in some way? If so, we'd love to hear about it. Sincere reviews on **Amazon** and **Goodreads** help readers find the right book they are looking for.

www.ingramcontent.com/pod-product-compliance
Lightning Source LLC
Chambersburg PA
CBHW060825050426
42453CB00008B/597